MW00652776

THIS TOO SHALL PASS

THIS TOO SHALL PASS

A STORY OF MAKING PEACE WITH NOW

JET MENDES

NEW DEGREE PRESS

COPYRIGHT © 2020 JET MENDES

All rights reserved.

THIS TOO SHALL PASS

A Story of Making Peace with Now

ISBN   978-1-64137-943-4 *Paperback*

            978-1-64137-749-2 *Kindle Ebook*

            978-1-64137-751-5 *Ebook*

To My Loving Family...

Mom, Dad, Paris, August, and Brice,
Uncle Jay, Uncle Bradley, Grandma Gloria,
Grandma Jean, and Grandpa Nate...
This book is for you.
To My Dear Friend Noah...
Cheers, Six.

JET'S
TABLE OF CONTENTS

———

"My destination is the here and now, the only time and place where true life is possible."

—THICH NHAT HANH

AUTHOR'S NOTE

The Great Recession of 2008 was only the beginning of a turbulence that suddenly shook my family. Afterward, I indignantly wondered what was so "great" about all of the tragedy that followed the collapse. It seems that there is more to learn from irony than I thought.

There are lessons to be learned from our recessions, both individual and global. There is also strength to be gained from the process of breaking down and rebuilding, from having to tap into resilience. In hardship, whether one believes so or not, there is peace.

There were times when my family and I wished to run from the pain, and it would certainly be the kind of running motivated by fear—the tireless kind you see in movies when the characters flee to escape some horrible villain. Plenty of times we thought of every way to escape but each of us had realized at one moment or another that the only way to overcome the source of threat was to stop running.

When there is courage, there is no longer any running from the fears we create for ourselves by having given them all kinds of names and frightening stories. By bringing ourselves closer to that fear, letting ourselves be more intimate, vulnerable, and non-judgmental with the nature of it, we strengthen our understanding of the truth and surprising harmlessness of what we perceived to be villainous by nature. When the running has stopped so, too, has the threatening chase. The fear subsides, and as it does, so does the presence of our self-made peril.

I believe Eckhart Tolle describes this notion best when he wrote:

You might say, "What a dreadful day," without realizing that the cold, the wind, and the rain or whatever condition you react to are not dreadful. They are as they are. What is dreadful is your reaction, your inner resistance to it, and the emotion that is created by that resistance. In Shakespeare's words, "There is nothing either good or bad, but thinking makes it so."[1]

I believe there's a prevalent misconception about confronting adversity. Before us now, there is a culture of escapism endemic to our world that has led to even more pain, anxiety, stress, and suffering. We are told that we are "fight or flight" creatures, and all too often it seems that we choose "flight." With frequency, we choose to run and hide from Universal gifts that arrive disguised as struggle. We have come to

---

1   Eckhart Tolle, *A New Earth: Awakening to Your Life's Purpose*, (London: Penguin, 2016).

perceive pain and discomfort as the most devastating facets of life, and we hold tight to a fear of what would happen should we choose to stand tall in the face of conflict. By doing so, we limit ourselves both in strength and spirit. The fear begets further fear, and in our attempts to escape the realities of the day, we create for ourselves a persistent anxiety. We jeopardize our own health in efforts to circumvent a struggle that has only come to better us.

To escape, we may bury ourselves into our phones, stripping ourselves from the Now and giving ourselves over to shallow comparisons and distractions from the divine moment before us. We may use drugs or alcohol to numb what we are meant to feel in attempt to eschew all that we have deemed as 'negative'. In this culture of addiction, we have become slaves to retail, relentlessly bombarded by the feeling of material want, whether it be for affirmation, belonging, self-worth, or any other means for egoic satiation. This addiction has caused us to live too many moments remiss of what is most important—the perfection of Now.

Through adopting the perspective of looking at struggle and challenge as a beautiful and natural offering of life, I feel that I've been able to find a gratitude so deep that at times it breaks me down into tears of joy. I have found that moments of egolessness enable our connection to the world in a way that leaves no room for fear or unhappiness. All that is required of us to create these moments is to remain unwaveringly in the present. However, it is much easier said than done.

To be present is to remove oneself from the ego, which I have come to learn is the source of all pain and unpleasantness. It is the ego that drives us toward fear, compares and complains, gossips and deprives us of appreciation, and attaches, identifies, and resists what is. It is the ego that distracts us from the beauty of Now and prohibits our growth. It is the ego that prohibits us from both loving and being loved. Each moment we dedicate to being present is an erosion of our ego and a step toward clarity. If we let ourselves be present during the times that we, our loved ones, or the world suffer, we strengthen both ourselves and the greater whole. By doing so, our suffering does not become selfish or victimized, but rather the very source of our healing.[2]

I have come to learn that the most divine things we are given in this life are often found through what we consider to be the most tragic. Tribulations, when worked through, give way to gratitude. Tears, when given the time to dry, give way to laughter. Hunger, when not met with indulgence, gives way to a sense of fulfillment. Insecurities are broken down and reshaped into courage and confidence. What we perceive as darkness will always give way to light should we choose to remain present long enough to see the sun rise.

I've written this book for everyone, including myself, who needs to be reminded of the beauty and perfection of the life that each of us have been given. This book is for kids of my generation and adjacent generations who seek some type of relief from the pressures of the day, and who may feel

---

2   Eckhart Tolle, *A New Earth: Awakening to Your Life's Purpose*, (London: Penguin, 2016).

misplaced or misguided. I've written this book for parents like mine who, with or without children, feel both the weight of responsibility on their shoulders and the same muddled passion for life that they felt as teenagers. For the parents who have just lost or found love in their life, who feel they have given up or given themselves over to their children. This book is for anyone who wants to listen and share more with the world. By reading this book, you grant us the opportunity to have an open conversation and relate to one another.

This book is for all of those in my family who surround me in spirit and for my family who I speak with regularly. It is for my friends who have been there to see these stories up close and have given more love and support than I could have ever dreamt of. You have given me life. I share this with you in hopes that you will find entertainment, empowerment, and possibly enlightenment through these stories.

You should read this book if you need a meditation, a deep breath, a cry, or a laugh. By reading this, you will hopefully find a new sense of peace and understanding within yourself. These are stories about the way in which life happens for us, never against us. By reading this book, I hope you'll realize that we all have the choice to live a life that is filled with joy and love, regardless of what arrives during our journey. Let us begin here, being present as we move along.

To you reading this, I say thank you and I love you.

PART ONE

THE EGO AND I

CHAPTER 1

NEAR MODERN DISASTER

———

In the living room of our home hung a large, radiant photograph, and although I was ten years old and knew nothing about art, I knew that this photograph was important to my father. The photograph depicted a family caught in a violent storm. They are on what looks to be a pier on an oceanfront, with hurricane-like winds raging. The storm is shown to be so strong that the pole in the picture is bending from the force of the wind and the woman, who I presume to be the mother of the child and wife of the man pictured, is on the ground holding onto this pole with every last ounce of her strength. Her life, evidently, depends on it.[3]

Meanwhile, the father is battling the wind, holding onto nothing but the hand of his young daughter, who is completely flying in air and clutching her dad's hand for dear life. The dad is leaned forward, trying to bully his way through

---

3   Nic Nicosia, "Near (Modern) Disaster #8," (MutualArt, 1984).

the wind the way a lineman drives through blocking pads for practice. He is hunkered down as best he can. In the background, there are several beach chairs flying wildly, caught in the storm's violent blow, and the whitewash of the waves appear to be forcefully rushing in. It looks like a modern vacation rendition of *The Tempest*. What's also fascinating about the photo is that the weather in the picture, other than the presence of this hurricane, seems to be pleasant.

I did not like the piece very much, even from the first moment that I saw it hung up. It was frightening and reminded me of the beach we would often visit in Florida. My ability to feel the piece on some kind of visceral level, to envision being in the photograph holding onto my dad's hand, evoked a great deal of fear. The photo had a verisimilitude, giving me the impression I was part of their struggle. This was not something I wanted to have to look at day after day the way I did.

My dad admired fine art and its surrounding culture even from a young age. Fascinated by the crowds and events garnered for its celebration, he found some kind of profound meaning in the inexplicable qualities of the work he saw at galleries and friends' homes. My father is a romantic like I am, and I say this because it leaves less room to misunderstand how it was rather easy for his curiosity to wander off into greater depths of the art world.

Out of college and working as a futures trader on the floor of the Chicago Mercantile Exchange, he began to feel the chasm narrow between him and this world. He still didn't really know the first thing about the art he was then seeing more frequently or the artists who had summoned up whatever necessary to create such work, but he was now in closer proximity to it. With art, he didn't have to know much to understand that he was in the presence of beauty, some more explicable than others. The more work he saw, the more the sensationalism of the artists' pursuit became, to him, palpable. He admired the undeniable and provocative devotion behind it all and the tacit understanding that these creations were, while representative of an array of different stories, all emblems of prosperity.

When Expo Chicago, which featured art, came to Navy Pier in 1982, he decided to take his father to see the show. The two of them meandered awhile but, as my father tells me, nothing seemed to move him on the visceral level he had anticipated until they came across Roy Lichtenstein's *The Sound Of Music*, a piece depicting a woman with short blond hair being struck by musical notes, as if they had flown off of a piece of sheet music and through her open window to be dispatched directly into her right-side temple.

This woman wears a charmed and almost mischievous grin, as though she is flirting or being flirted with. Either way, there is an element of flirtation in this work, and her eyes, directed at the presumable source of music, gleam from the natural light coming through the window. Half of her face is warmly lit by this natural light, while the other half, in a symbolic kind of obviousness pointing toward something which I do not pretend to know, is a darker, somewhat arctic shade of blue. The two hues of her face—the endearing duality of warm and cold—are separated by a black bordering region of shade that runs from the top of her head to the bottom of her chin.

It is, in many ways, a romantic composition, something that appeals to the pleasantness of humanity. It is, in the traditional Lichtenstein style, a work of pop art that radiates a comic book-like exuberance for life. Even if you knew nothing about it, it is difficult to see Lichtenstein's work without planting your feet and staring for a while, mesmerized by its glow.

Of the many people I'm sure this piece had an effect on, my dad was one who so impacted that he grabbed the attention of a liaison working the expo to inquire about it. The woman enlightened my father on Lichtenstein's background, his personal and professional life, and his style of work.

My dad looked to my grandpa for a brief, unspoken approval of what was to come next and, so the story goes, my grandpa was on board.

"How much for this one?" my dad asked her.

"Three hundred seventy-five," she replied.

"Three hundred seventy-five? Great, I'll take it!" My father told her.

"Really?"

She asked with what must have been studied suspicion, and yet the fleeting thought that this young man, in his tucked button-down and bold-framed prescription glasses, might actually be serious.

"Yes. Three hundred seventy-five dollars, no problem."

"Sir, that's my fault for not being clearer. The price is three hundred seventy-five *thousand* dollars."

This was the day that my father came to understand the value of fine art.

For reference, Roy Lichtenstein's most expensive work titled *Masterpiece* sold for 165 million dollars in 2017. I own a twenty-dollar rendition that hangs in my room here at school.

After that day at Expo Chicago, my father got in touch with the curator of a local gallery, whom he had known because the man happened to be his neighbor at the time, and asked whether he'd be willing to tutor my father on the subject of fine art.

The following year, with a broader knowledge and appreciation, my father returned to Art Expo again with his father, but this time he did not leave empty handed. That day he bought his first work of art, created by a Swiss painter named Luciano Castelli. It was a painted portrait of Luciano's girlfriend at the time.

Now, the entirety of the walls in our home were covered with art of all kinds. There were photographs that seemed to capture real people doing real things, and there were paintings that did not. Many works consisted of shapes and blends of colors, even things that lit up, such as one photograph of an enormous golden pistol flying through the sky with hundred-dollar bills as wings. Outside, there were sculptures scattered about the several acres surrounding the house and in the very center of our driveway, the black pavement circumventing the art as if it had also learned not to touch, were a large pair of fists that sat beside each other, each of them clenched as if grasping onto something or preparing for a fight.

In the music room of our basement stood a giant sculpture of a man holding a trumpet. He was surrounded by a drum set, a keyboard, and other instruments that were not art and could be played on occasion with youthful and slovenly fervor. This man appeared as though he was a band member perpetually waiting for the rest of the ensemble to arrive while he warmed up. He stood alone amongst these instruments. He wore a light blue suit, a thick mustache, and a tilted fedora, and his cheeks were puffed out in passionate exhalation. He seemed to put all the breath he had into that trumpet.

I did not know these "installations" weren't to be touched or sat on or used as obstacles for soccer drills because they just sat around like everything else in our home. I could not discern any real difference between the installations and the kitchen chairs per se, but my parents made it a point to walk my sister and I through the house in a way that felt like we were touring a park and explained, in one manner or another, that the pieces were not to be touched.

Part of me liked learning about what ought to be valued and respected, and when my friends came over, I would occasionally explain to them, the same way my dad explained to me, why one piece couldn't be touched and why the other couldn't be sat on. I believe this helped satiate my voracious hunger to be "mature."

"This is very expensive and very delicate so please don't play with this, okay honey?" my mother would say, hoping for any kind of assurance I understood and would not make some kind of grand, costly mistake. It seemed that I had been born to make those kinds of mistakes, that my life was just one giant effort to overcome that cursed quality. My mother explained the factor of expenses: she talked to us about the cost of these items. My father, on the other hand, explained them to us like they were living beings. He cautioned us to be weary of how we lived with them in the same way that we were told how to behave with other students at recess, "Treat others the way you'd like to be treated—with respect."

To this day, he still reminds me of this, and to this day, I still tell him that I hear him and understand.

"I know you may want to, but don't grab his arm here. He's very delicate and you could hurt him, and we don't want that," my father said about the man with the trumpet.

I understood. I wasn't dumb; I was ten—nearly a man in the Jewish community—and I wanted to behave like it, even though it was tough to do so a lot of the time.

I wasn't enthralled with most of the art as it was, which I believe was conducive to the requisite of caution. I seldom felt the impulse to touch or examine the art because it did not appeal to me the way my trampoline or miniature soccer ball did.

Either way, I came to understand that the photograph of this family who I did not know but deeply sympathized with, who I feared would not make it out of that storm, meant something to my father because it hung in the living room. This was the room where our family spent the most time, and it acted as a focal point in our home. This is where we would spend weekends hanging around and weeknights watching movies and cartoons. It was the room we saw most, and this photograph was intentionally selected to be hung in this room, meaning that my parents favored it more than others. Something drew my father to this piece. Something in it had an everyday kind of appeal to him. If our home was a gallery, which it certainly was to a degree, this photo had been put on display in the main room with intent.

Like all galleries, there comes a time when it must be shut down, when the art is taken off of the walls and the lights are shut off. The art is either kept or sold, stolen, or recirculated back into the world some other way, but at the end of the day, it all must go elsewhere. The time comes when the doors to the gallery are locked, and the owners, now the owners no longer, are left without a key.

CHAPTER 2

HOME DIVIDED

———

The assets we shared as a family began to dissipate from our possession back into the economy. My father's investment in SOGO, or South of Ogden Chicago, with efforts to turn the neighborhood into an arts district, deteriorated during the collapse of the housing market in 2008. I was young— still not yet in junior high school—when he was working on this development and did not know that this project had been draining him of his energy and financial health for years. I did not ask questions, and on the rare occasion I did, all questions were met with ephemeral and ambiguous optimism. My father spoke in an aphoristic species of code. He'd say things like "It is what it is" or "Let's put it this way: there are no shortcuts in life," followed by some form of an enlightened smile.

His refusal to remove the mask of positivity was so tirelessly stubborn that we could not remember what he looked like without it.

My mom would periodically mock him.

"Everything's great with Steve! Everything is just fine and dandy!"

She would tease him with names like Sunny Steve, accusing him of living in a world he had created for himself, a world which he maintained for the sake of others where the sun was always shining. The older I got, the more I realized that his presentation of optimism wasn't so much for others as it was for the sake of his family. Simply put, he did not want his family to worry about "things." He assured us that "things" were taken care of, and Paris and I had an unwavering faith in him, as we still do, but our mother grew less and less convinced.

She was angry with him, that much I understood. She said it was a waste of his energy, and it was disingenuous of him to act the way he did. She used it as a topic of lecture for my sister and I, telling us not to be afraid to express when things got bad—to not hide it—and that "it" was a dangerous mechanism to use in the long-lasting game of mental health.

"Don't stuff your emotions," she'd say.

I would come to learn, much later, how right she was about that, and this "it" she spoke of was the pain each of us carried. When this pain arrived, it needed to be both accepted and confronted through the recognition of whatever it brought, if we did not want it to become a permanent part of our lives.

At that age, I often held back my tears because I had never seen my dad cry and assumed I shouldn't either. While fighting back tears, I could feel myself choking on a plum-like lump in my throat. My mom would tell me privately that it wasn't healthy to hold my tears back, and I shouldn't be like my dad and hold everything in because it closes off my throat chakra. I didn't know what a throat chakra was, but I assumed it was related to the plum I felt.

My sister and I would often go with our dad to visit the buildings he had bought in their developmental stages: big and cavernous buildings with hallow and dusty insides. We were told to be careful whilst playing inside; stray nails, splintered wood, and loud power tools laid dormant around these buildings like some kind of boneyard.

"Just wait and see how cool this will all become," my father would say to me and Paris.

He'd explain the development plan for each building, even though it was tough to envision how something so desolate could become full and beautiful. *That must take hundreds of years*, I thought in fleeting disbelief while my father walked me through a building that would soon become a theater and another that would become a communal art gallery.

Santi, the head of the construction team at one of the main buildings, had six sons—plus a wife who I never got to meet—and these were Paris and my playmates during our time spent there. Santi was an older Mexican man who had a mystical quality, similar to that which cinema likes to create around actors like Morgan Freeman. It's a modern, prophet-like quality. There was a glare of wisdom in Santi's eye that I could see, even from a young age, though I couldn't quite describe it. Then again, I believe that may be part of the societal appeal around characters like this—one with a certain indescribable quality amongst a culture of labels and categories and descriptions. Santi was simply a sanctified figure, someone you needed to meet.

His sons were young and close in age, and they seemed no different than myself; they just wanted to run around and play like I did. The singular, rather obvious disparity between us was that their English was not as strong as the kids I went to school with. I did my best to use the Spanish I was learning from kids on my soccer team. I made an honest effort to explain the rules of hide and seek to the boys.

"Y tú a la izquierda," I offered, hoping they knew what I meant and that I wasn't embarrassing myself which, surely, I was.

One of Santi's sons, who the brothers called Pollo, was autistic. I couldn't help but watch him constantly. I looked at him and felt a throbbing pain in my heart. I could feel in my throat and stomach the heaviness that comes before you start crying. It pained me that he was, from what I had learned in school and from my family, "disabled" or "special needs." I talked to Pollo, but I wasn't quite sure how to go about it, so I spoke as though I was speaking with someone younger than I was. That's how I saw his brothers engage with him. They would speak to him in a delicate tone and sometimes place their hand on his back when they explained something. If they were leaving, they might grab his hand and guide him out, not necessarily because he needed actual guidance to be taken from place to place, but because his brothers cared for him. It was something more than what can be learned in school; brotherly behavior was deeply biological, primitive even. We take care of our own by nature. This was one of the ways they showed love for Pollo.

There was a fragility to Pollo's existence, and maybe that's what broke my heart. I had this idea that he couldn't play or live in the same capacity that we seemed to. I thought that no one deserved that type of life, and I held onto a quiet anger for the bigger, wickedly unfair force that had done this to him. One of the days we were at the building, Pollo began crying for some unknown reason. Three of his brothers quickly began consoling him back to equanimity, and at this moment, I learned just how voyeuristic of a creature I was. I could not look away from him, even when I told myself I should. I could feel my heart becoming inflated with a piercing heat as I watched, and I was sure that in only a matter of moments I would feel some kind of balloon-like pop in my chest.

I watched until I felt myself about to burst into tears. I did not want to cry in front of all of these kids, especially not after they had just worked so diligently and gracefully to extinguish the tears of their brother mere moments ago. I couldn't handle the pressure in my heart anymore. I held it in and waited until I got to the car before breaking down. I cried nearly the whole ride home, explaining to my dad how bad I felt for them. I felt not just for Pollo but for the whole family whose life seemed to revolve around caring for this fragile boy, and I thought they too must cry because of it.

Soon my father stopped bringing my sister and I to these same buildings, and I did not see Santi or Pollo anymore. My dad was so confident about his idea for the arts district that he became too stubborn to forsake his already-invested time and dedication. I watched my mother become more and more upset, and the fights between them became more frequent. My mother feared for the future of our family while my father did his best to remain sturdy through this storm that seemed to grow fiercer by the day.

My father's composure, coupled with his stubborn confidence, only fueled the flames of my mother's anger. While he did his best to stand tall and weather the storm, my mother decided to run for her own life and the lives of her children. It had become clear that the raft we were on as a family, the life of security and comfort we had been sharing all this time, now had a gaping hole in the bottom. My mother was not ready to drown. She refused to give up everything she loved, and she explained to my sister and I that the three of us would be getting off this raft together. Our father would be fine, but there was a waterfall on the near horizon, and he fancied himself a boatsman, albeit, in her eyes, a foolishly fearless one.

The truth was my father may have even saw himself as more powerful than the impending waterfall. But what he failed to realize, which did not become obvious to him until later, was that there is no strength greater than that of Mother Nature. Any man who sees himself as stronger than the force of nature is a man bound to become an example of otherwise.

One night, as we sat around the kitchen table, my father gone probably on a drive or a walk or leaned up against a hidden wall silently crying somewhere, my mother explained to Paris and me that she and my father would be separating. The three of us would be moving out of our home, which we had come to love and appreciate as the home that raised us, where friends and family gathered for meals and holidays, and where we slept and ate and shared life together. Now, suddenly, none of this would be possible anymore. This was seismic news, the world beneath me stirring violently as though it were being painfully woken up. Subsequently, I filled with a kind of grief that felt like thousands of plates and glasses being hurled across the house, shattering and spitting themselves back upward wildly.

My mother found another home that she made my sister and I tour with heavy-footed reluctance. It wasn't far, but it seemed darker and much smaller than our real home. Neither Paris nor I liked the idea of moving into this house, but the truth was we really had no say in where we were going to live. My mom bought the house with money her grandma gifted her, and a week later, we were moving in.

My mom's grandfather, alongside his brother, founded what would become a prominent American screen-printing company in the late forties, and at one point even worked closely with Andy Warhol, although the world wasn't nearly as familiar with Warhol as they would become years later. One of the known familial anecdotes is that Warhol gifted my great-grandfather three of his pieces after they finished up their work together. Shortly after deciding Warhol's art was not aesthetically pleasing, my great grandpa threw them away. Nice move, grandpa!

We moved our possessions into this new house while my dad was left to live on his own for a week before he would have to move out of our home. Years later, when I was mature enough to expect an honest response, I asked my dad what it was like to have to sleep there, the house barren after his family had moved out. He told me those were the worst few days of his life. It made the cancer he fought in his earlier years seem like a day spent at the park. He told me that, to this day, he has never cried as hard as he did that first night there alone.

At the time, my sister and I couldn't quite conceive how big of a deal this was for my dad. We figured we were just a few minutes away, and it was not like we were moving out of the state. The truth was we couldn't begin to grasp the suffering he had to endure at that time. That week, while my father stayed in the house, the bank had come to take any art that was of significant value, along with the house itself. They came to take the life my father had created with his bare hands—by throwing them emphatically and decisively into the air in all kinds of variations as floor traders do—as he stood there, palms open, with no choice but to surrender. The fists in the driveway put up no fight either, thrown in the back of some big truck and driven off, never to be seen again.

The bank dismounted the photograph in our living room of the family withstanding strong winds, which must have been the only thing I was glad to see go. My dad turned in our swift and lustrous cars for a dilapidated Jeep. After he turned in the keys to the house, he moved into a friend's home who was away for a few months on work.

I slept there one night, a massive home that seemed desolate of any light or food, and assumed it was our new home, but my father eventually explained we would only be staying there for a little while before we found a permanent, new home together. He assured me everything would be fine, but I could feel the heaviness in his heart when he spoke. I felt an exhausted uneasiness I had never seen in my father before. There was not much sun in him now.

One day I was playing in the driveway of this house with a friend of mine. We were kicking the soccer ball around and when I gave it a good boot, the ball lifted off the ground and hit the lamp that sat above the driveway gate, shattering it into hundreds of pieces. My father heard the sound and immediately came out to see what I had done. That broken lamp was the last straw.

"What the fuck are you doing!"

This was the first time my dad ever cursed at me. His voice, delivered low and stern, rumbled as thunder does, and the graveness with which his eyes gleamed struck me down right there in the driveway. For a moment, I did not know the man who yelled at me. My father, who had always been in the mood to joke and keep things lighthearted, was now bearing the weight of a frustration that was both frigid and dense.

After a few weeks of my dad living in that house, he moved into a one thousand square foot condo that barely had enough hot water to get me through a quick shower. The kitchen, dining room, and living room were just one collective, larger room. I know now that for many, this is a luxury, but for me, at this time, it was a source of intense perturbation.

I was twelve years old, and although I believed I had developed a comprehensive grasp of our new circumstances, I still couldn't fathom the conditions in which my dad was now living. However, as bad as I felt for my dad, I didn't feel comfortable staying at his house because being there came with the perceivably impossible task of swallowing the reality that was being pushed down our throats. The battered and claustrophobic feel of his condo made my mother's house feel like a mansion. The space and comfort of her new house left no contest when deciding whose house would become home and whose would become secondary. Thus came the birth of two separate entities: "home" and "dad's house." Shortly after, my father began his efforts to eliminate the gap between the two.

CHAPTER 3

BATTLE OF BUDS

———

About a year after we moved into my mother's house, she began dating a man named Tim who was, in almost every way, the exact opposite of my father.

Tim rode loud motorcycles and wore bracelets and lifted weights, and he dressed like a rebellious college kid with a fervent affinity for rock 'n' roll culture. My father wore suits and ties even when he was not going to work, rode bicycles, and donned no other jewelry than a watch on his left wrist.

Tim carried with him a dark, heavy hubris which manifested most noticeably in the way he walked with his chest puffed up and led the rest of his body.

The moment I met him in a Jamba Juice, before I even knew he and my mother were seeing each other, I felt an uneasiness in my gut. I did not like the way he looked at my mother when they spoke. In his presence, I felt the arousal of something deeply territorial.

I began to see him more frequently, sometimes even at our house, and the more I saw him the more I felt the flame of abhorrence grow wild and hot.

Of course, in the early stages of their relationship he did his best to behave courteously, talking in that "buddy" tone with Paris and I and offering my mother nice things. Even at that age, I could see past it. I think we are all born with the inherent ability to detect what is genuine and what is not. Some call it intuition and others don't bother to label it but, nevertheless, they know that this intuitive, radar-like device is there to wield. Some choose to ignore it, taking the batteries out and putting their trust elsewhere. I, however, did not.

Soon, it was easy to notice when my mother was upset about their relationship. He or she had done or said something they shouldn't have or made each other feel guilty about something they should have done but didn't—like why my mother couldn't make us like him and why we never spent time with him. It was obvious when he'd press her with these kinds of concerns because afterward, she'd come home and complain to us about why we refused to integrate him into our lives.

"Why can't you just be nice to him for my sake?"

The irony was that she never seemed to understand the reason we did not treat him kindly was, in fact, entirely for her sake.

My mother had been raised by a father who abused her and it became clear, after almost ten years of being with my father who never once laid a hand on her—one of the facts she had adulated when she'd lecture Paris and I on what kind of relationship to look for later in life—that was the execrable form of love she was reverting to.

That was the love she felt she then, for incomprehensible reasons, deserved.

After about a year of dating, their relationship was teeming with rancid energy from toxicity and abuse, but still she pleaded for us to be kind to him, to spend time and share dinners with him.

"I'm not going over there."

"Jet, don't be ridiculous. We're just going for dinner quick and then we'll leave. We'll be in and out."

"I'm not going."

"Jet. You don't have a choice. He's been very generous with us and it doesn't look good that you never want to talk to him. He really feels like you hate him."

"He's got a strong intuition."

"Jet, please. Do it for me. I promise we'll be there for forty minutes, at most."

It was never just forty minutes. I'd have to put on my "nice guy" act, making conversation with him and his son, who was a few years younger than me. I had trouble deciding whether to despise the kid solely for being the son of this man I so deeply detested, or if he was his own person who didn't deserve to be hated because of something he couldn't control. After all, he had never done my mother nor I any wrong. My ego told me to hurt him to bring indirect pain to his father. I decided against doing so because every fiber of my being knew that Tim's son did not deserve wickedness.

Tim would stare at me across the table as my mother or I spoke, knowing, challenging, like we were battling for my mother's love. It was clear he believed he was winning.

The more I saw him, the more I wanted to get physically stronger. My focus in class began drifting toward fantasies of us fighting and me saying something blunt and serrated about him and his family.

I started working out almost every day, using these aggressive thoughts as a source of energy. He and I worked out at the same gym, which meant there were many days when we were working out at the same time. On these days, I would exercise harder than I probably should have, walking around the gym after a few sets of an exercise like a peacock flaring my colors as a means of intimidation.

He'd typically walk over at some point, chest puffed, and say hello, looking at the weight I was lifting with unspoken condescension. We were animals facing off.

After being gone for a night, my mother came home with bruises on her arms. When I asked what happened, she told me that she fell off a bicycle—she was never a good liar—but the truth couldn't have been more obvious.

The thought of him putting his hands on my mother kept me awake with tempestuous anger. It got me out of bed at unreasonable hours of the night to do push-ups beside my bed.

It was the summer going into my senior year and, in my mind, I was big and tall now. I'd come into my mom's room often while she was in bed writing or watching television, or into the kitchen if she was making food, with my shirt off and say:

"Hey ma, am I lookin' big or what?" I'd flex and stand up extra tall.

She always got a kick out of this.

"Yes, you're massive. I'm surprised you even fit through the doors anymore."

"Me too. That reminds me, I think I'm gonna need a new bedroom door 'cause my shoulders are getting too damn wide!"

She'd crack up and then suddenly become more serious.

"Jet, did you send those pictures into the modeling agencies like I told you?"

"Not yet, ma. I'm gonna do that this week."

"Do it today. You need to start getting paid for those looks."

"Yeah yeah, I hear you, mom! I will in a sec."

Weeks later, after forgetting to submit pictures to these agencies, she got fed up and told me she wouldn't let me back into the house until I took the train into the city and walked around from agency to agency with my novice headshots and a perfunctorily prepared monologue. I went to five different "open calls," which is essentially a tryout but solely based on looks, before returning home proud of having crossed that task off of the list.

I was rejected from every agency I went to that week for one reason or another—I have yet to see the day wherein I receive payment for "those looks".

A few days later, my mom had just left the house for a grocery run while I moved some boxes that needed to be taken from our garage and down into our basement.

I heard a car pull up, the door open and close, and I saw Tim walking up the driveway. The ripples of summer heat diluted my vision of him as he approached. In my mind, I could hear the old western duel whistle. And I could feel the sun watching, pressing down on my skin doggedly.

I was thankful that my shirt was off and that I had just been moving heavy objects so the blood in my veins was already pumping. He stopped a few feet short of me, but then, impulsively, I moved closer.

"Hey bud."

I couldn't stand him calling me "bud."

"Is your mom here?"

I took a step closer, my face just inches from his, with my shoulders back and chest out.

"She's not."

There was a moment of silence as we both stared at each other, my synapses uproarious in their encouragement to take a swing; I envisioned what would happen if my fist connected with his temple, and how that might even kill him, which gave way to thinking about the very real consequences of that outcome. These thoughts were the sober, levelheaded friend intervening before a sloppy bar fight.

"Okay, tell her I came by, will you?"

"Will do," I said, gritting my teeth.

Another moment was spent standing there looking at each other unflinchingly before he retreated to his car. I stood there flexing, my heart nearly beating through my chest.

Evidently, Tim told my mother about our interaction because the next day my mother asked me if I had tried to fight him.

"No. I just needed him to know he wasn't welcome here," I said.

After several more capricious months, I was sent to his house to return the wedding ring he had given my mom.

I'd never been so excited to run an "errand" in my life as I was to return that ring. My ego savored the taste of retaliation.

I wore a smirk on my face loaded with contempt when I showed up to his door.

I knocked, not sure who would answer, but in a moment, he was standing before me.

I held out the small box.

"Here's that ring, *bud*," I said.

I had rehearsed this line the entire drive over.

He took the ring out of the case and examined it, evidently making sure it was the one he gave my mother and he wasn't being tricked or making sure we hadn't pawned off the real one and purchased a knock-off to return to him.

While he examined it, his friend pulled up on a motorcycle. He and this guy were like Thing One and Thing Two. They may as well have been twins.

"Is this your backup?" I said slyly.

He looked up, visibly furious.

"Yeah, where's your fucking backup?" he spit back.

"Don't need any, *bud*."

I could feel my throat beginning to close from adrenaline. I walked off the front step, leaving him and his friend to do what they pleased with the ring, and got back in my car.

For a moment, I was pleased with how this scene played out in almost exact accordance with the way I envisioned it, but this satisfaction quickly subsided into violent feelings of disgust with myself.

CHAPTER 4

CHRIST, CANDLES, AND KIPPAHS

My mother was glad to have my friends over at the house, typically offering them a home-cooked meal and, if it was the weekend, allowing us a few beers, which my friends and I always commended her for, but I believe what people appreciated most about my mother was the warmth she naturally exuded. It was her warmth that made people feel welcome at our home.

Her maternal instincts were intense, ingrained deeply into the very fiber of her being, and, for as long as I can remember, she had been appointed by the community as an extended caretaker. If she heard someone in the neighborhood was sick—a friend, a neighbor, a teacher, our bank teller—she'd spring into action. She would send me to school with remedies for my friends when they were under the weather or to someone's house with a care package. She found self-healing through healing others.

At home, we had a giant cabinet full of homeopathic remedies ready to go at a moment's notice for any sort of pain or ailment.

Health was, as my mother saw it, the determining factor of one's quality of life and the essence of our existence.

I'll never forget when she found a pack of Orbit gum in my car. It went something like this:

"Jet, what the fuck is this?" I was driving and not looking. When I did turn, I saw she was holding up the pack of gum like it was a bag of cocaine.

"Gum," I said charmingly.

"Don't tell me you've been chewing this shit."

"I had one piece, ma. I just needed to grab a pack before I went out the other night."

"So, you bought a pack of fucking chemicals? Pull over."

"What?" I asked, in disbelief of her disappointed at that moment.

"Pull over. Right here."

I pulled over and she got out of the car with the pack of gum and threw it in the trash can at the end of a random driveway. She hopped back into the car.

"Don't ever let me catch you with that shit again."

"Okay, mom."

Now, I was having a good laugh.

"I mean it!" she said.

There was a brief moment of silence before I saw a smile come across her face.

"You should write a skit about this. It would be hysterical!"

In accordance with her philosophies about good health, exercising became a primary avenue through which we shared our time together.

She and I used to walk regularly down a trail that began right across the street from our house on Lorenzi Lane. The trail is about a mile long and its pavement stretches right to the shore of Lake Michigan. We would walk the path during all seasons, carrying our feet through the snow, kicking through the crisp leaves of autumn, and tiptoeing atop its naked warmth in the summer. We loved navigating through the summer air while the sun permeated our shoulders and sweat rolled innocuously down our tan necks more than anything. Side by side while we walked, I often couldn't help but notice how much taller than her I had become.

This observation never failed to turn my memory back to when I was eight years old or so. Every night before I went to bed, she'd walk me from her room to mine; we'd walk side by side down the hallway, my arm extended as high up as it could go to place my hand on her shoulder. This was a personalized metric system I used to measure my growth.

"You're gonna be big and tall one day. Don't you worry, my love," she'd say before scooping me up and throwing me onto her back. "Soon I'm not gonna be able to carry you! Oh, how I'm going to miss that!"

As I got older, she often expressed what sounded more like a request than a wish that I'd grow to be six feet tall. There was not a single thing she asked of me throughout her life that I seemed to be able to neglect—I grew to be six feet on the dot.

I watched her now, during my high school years, still carrying on with undeniable strength but visibly a more delicate creature. She who had once appeared invincible now revealed otherwise, and every time she threw her arms around my waist or arm as we walked, I was reminded of time gone by, and the changes that came with it.

My mother had begun her battle before I was even born. In her twenties, she had slammed her breast in a car door, which caused her initial round with breast cancer. After undergoing that first surgery to remove the tumor in her left breast, the cancer was supposed to be conquered with ease and become nothing more than a slight road bump on the path to a long and healthy life. However, that is not what happened.

What happened was the surgeon failed to perform a frozen section on her breast—a "frozen section" is a procedure most often used in oncological surgery to remove cancerous tissue— removing the larger tumor in the breast while unintentionally leaving behind a pea-sized tumor that, over the years, metastasized and became the source of my mother's over-twenty-year battle with breast, brain, bone, lung, and lymphatic cancer.

Naturally, there had been many doctors along the way who "regretted to inform" her that she only had several months to live. Naturally, she told every one of them otherwise. Surely enough, she outlived every medical estimate by about ten years. My mother was someone who only did things her way, especially when it came to her health.

I remember coming home from school one day and noticing a big pot full of organic soil on our kitchen table.

"Ma, what's going on in here? Are we gardening in the kitchen now?"

She called down from upstairs, "No, honey! Those are my sprouts. They're great for the kidneys!"

They began to grow fresh right there on our kitchen table, and when we'd sit down to eat, she'd pick a handful right out of the soil, give them a quick rinse, and add them to her dinner. I had become so accustomed to having to try everything that I wasn't even fazed when she offered. She threw a few pinches onto my plate.

If you look in my fridge today, it's very likely you'd find a box of fresh sprouts in there.

Not long after high school began, I had kids trying to buy and trade the lunches my mom made for me.

"Here's half a turkey sandwich, ya filthy animal. Throw me your pretzels," I'd say to my buddy Jonah a few times a week.

My mother would rise with the sun, make herself a bowl of cereal, and then craft my lunch for the day. By the time I got downstairs, my lunch would be ready and packed in a small to-go bag. It was like receiving a gift every weekday, each lunch a pleasant surprise. I cherished my mother's food, and to me it was an invaluable token of her love.

After my freshman year of high school, she began to undergo treatments and surgeries more regularly, which meant I had to begin packing my own lunch. And when I got my license, I frequently found myself making and dropping off meals to her at the hospital while she underwent treatment.

I was quick to decide that I did not like hospitals. Everything about them set me on edge, from the blinding radiance of the lights to the barrenness of the white interior, to the protective masks emblematic of some kind of life-threatening procedure, and to even the crinkling sounds of the doctor's pants as they speed walked through the squeaking, freezingly bright halls. Worst of all, I disliked having to walk by all of the other rooms on my way to where my mother was, glancing in at the other patients who were, to an obvious degree, not well.

To me, my mother was perfectly well. I perceived her visits to the hospital to be as harmless as a trip to the hair salon.

Her appointments, and even most of the surgeries, felt like routine maintenance because she made it feel that way. Even though she needed regular medical attention, she seemed perpetually unbreakable.

The more I was at the hospital, the more I became acquainted with the medical staff. From my perspective, doctors had always just been doctors the same way that teachers seemed to only be teachers when I was younger. In third grade, it was unimaginable my math teacher had any other life outside of who he was in the classroom. At that time, I imagined these teachers taught during the school day and slept at the school—possibly in some separate dormitory building—when the day was over. But I had become familiar with the staff at our local hospital—they became like extended family to us. As my mom and I walked the halls together, she'd frequently introduce me to the personnel:

"Diane, this is my big handsome boy," and I'd smile and extend my hand.

I couldn't help but anticipate, with excitement, the classic: *"Wow, you look just like your mother!"*

When people told me I looked like her, I felt I understood myself a little bit better. I found clarity in the thought of who I was in relation to what I was made up of. As I see it, one cannot totally understand a flower without first understanding the seeds and the soil from which it grew.

At the hospital, people, even staff, looked at her like she was a celebrity or some mythical legend. The way people reacted to her presence was cinematic at its core. All kinds of people, scattered about the peripheral, became like extras on the set of a movie in which my mother was the lead.

"There goes Dena! How does she still look like that after all of *that*?"

As much as I don't like the hospital, the truth is that being there with her helped me realize that my mother was my hero, and I felt foolish for having discovered that only after so many years shared together.

I would look over at her intermittently while we walked and smile with pride for the way she carried herself. In my eyes, she was a superhero without a cape. Walking down that path by our house, she'd occasionally stop and let a smile find her face, and look up directly towards the sun, letting out an "Ahhhhhh" of appreciation. I'd smile and continue walking, she'd catch up, and then we'd be walking in stride. We'd walk past the man with the long gray hair who always sat on the same bench with his beagle, smoking a cigar. The dog was never on a leash, but they would both just sit there, perfectly still as though in meditation, staring at the green hill in front of them.

"How are you?" I'd say to them every time.

"We're alright, thank you," the man would say, answering on behalf of both him and his beagle.

There was a running joke between my mother and I about our anticipation of the day when the beagle, cigar in mouth, would be the one to respond for the both of them. The man would then say something like, "Hey Bucko, that's my line!"

The smell of the man's cigar was fantastic and blended in with the summer air perfectly.

My mother and I walked at the exact same pace, fast and light, but sometimes in a lingering manner when she wanted to stop and appreciate a tree or a smell. This could be enough for the both of us, just being able to live and breathe and play outside in the clean heat. We were alike in that way. Sometimes she'd pump her arms up and down while exhaling a burst of audible breath that sounded like "shh" with each pump of the arm. I believe it was something she learned in a tai chi or dahn yoga class. Paris and I would always tease her until we felt we had succeeded in bringing the "shhh"s to an end, but she'd just start right back up again because she really just didn't give a damn.

She'd meet our complaining with total disregard:

"Oh, shut up! You kids are always so embarrassed by everything!"

It seemed that, many years ago, my mom had lost all sense of what it felt to be embarrassed. She did everything with unwavering confidence. This, I found, even included the way that she walked. She simply would not budge toward submission or conformity for the sake of what someone else may have wanted from her.

Once we made it to the lake, we would sit down on a bench that looked right out into the water and take a few seconds to digest the view, the blends of blue where the water met the sky and the limitlessness of them both. The sounds of the waves kissing the sand and rocks would bring our eyes to a close. We would sit there, eyes shut, inhaling and exhaling as the water did, and I'd like to imagine she expressed silent gratitude to The Universe for my sister and I, for making her strong and capable, for the sun and the water and the wind and the trees, and for putting her where she was supposed to be in the world. I listened some more to the water and gave my attention over to the smooth breeze that tickled my neck before taking the next few moments to thank The Universe for my family and friends, for our health, for Its unadulterated guidance and protection, for the sun and the water and the wind and the trees, and for putting me where I was supposed to be in the world. I promised The Universe that I would trust Its agenda, for that agenda is also innately mine.

We opened our eyes to the brightness of the same gorgeous summer day.

"I got so lucky to have a son like you."

I would joke and reply, "I know," and then thank her with a quiet sincerity.

"Have I told you I loved you yet today? And that you're handsome?"

"Not yet, I don't think."

"Well, you're handsome and I love you."

I would thank her like an embarrassed son, but I loved when she told me that. When she said things like that, it made me picture how the two of us would lay in bed together when I was much younger, and she'd say:

"Goodnight chachi, I love you"

I'd whisper back, "Goodnight momma, love you."

But she would keep laying there because she didn't want to leave me. "No, no, no, 'tis I who loves you."

I'd laugh and return, "Oh no, no, 'tis I who loves you."

We'd keep going until both of us were laughing and she'd put my energy at ease with quiet warmth and adoration, leaving sometime after I had fallen into a deep, innocent sleep.

Naturally, that innocence faded. By my junior and senior year of high school, I began waking up to a hostile home more often. My mother or sister would need something done, and newer, bigger bills were coming. Questions about where the money from my dad was and why we hadn't gotten any arose, with my mom reminding us that she pays for everything. The years of medication, especially recently, had not helped any of this. Some mornings I would wake up and the tension within the house would be tangible; I knew from the noises of things being moved around the house or from raised voices that as soon as I walked out of my room, I was stepping into a war zone. As soon as my mom and Paris heard footsteps, I was met with a "Jet!" *Fuck.*

"Yeah?" I'd ask innocuously, with full knowledge of the unloading that was about to take place.

"Jet, get your ass down here and take out this garbage right now, and did you call that woman at The Second City like I asked you to? Of course you didn't. Go drop off this breakfast to the Steins and make sure you get my bowls back when you're there, and then come home. There's things I need you to do."

My mother had many friends and clients who used her as a personal chef and wellness counselor, and while my sister was my mother's chief assistant, I was her delivery boy. I didn't mind because it was easy work and a perfect way to get out of the house.

Two steps into the house upon my return and Paris would say:

"Jet, I need you to run to the bank to deposit this check and go to Whole Foods with this list, but not the Deerfield Whole Foods, the Glenview one, because the Deerfield one doesn't have bone marrow. We gotta make food for Lisa today."

My sister Paris is two years older and may very well be the most responsible human being I've ever met. She helped run my mother's wellness brand shortly after she began high school, and at around the same time, she came into her role as my mother's best friend, and eventually her primary caretaker.

My mother constantly affirmed Paris' aptitude, telling her that she'd run a Fortune 500 company when she was older because she's "big and tall and smart and beautiful."

"Why do you always say 'big'? I lost four pounds this month!"

"Paris, I'm not calling you fat! You're just big boned and beautiful like Madonna's daughter!" This comment only made things worse.

"Madonna's daughter is ugly!" Paris would retort.

I had watched this scene time and time again and told myself I would be the one to convince Paris of her beauty, because it was obvious to me that she really was beautiful and that she deserved to know.

From the moment I was born, Paris called me her "baby."

"Baby, come here baby! Come here to sissy," she could be heard saying frequently on our home video tapes from when we were young, and everything seemed worthy of documenting to our parents.

It was always my mom's voice behind the camera saying something like:

"Kids, where are we?" or "Jet, come here and show us your moves!" or "Steve, what do you have to say to the camera?" My dad would always say something like:

"Uhh well let me just say how beautiful it is to be here… uhh and I'm grateful to be alive and healthy."

"Very nice, Steve. Okay finish eating your breakfast."

Paris would come running in from somewhere off screen yelling and whining, "I see it!"

Her hands were extended out, desperately reaching for the camera, wanting to wield the power of recording. Every so often, my mom would give Paris the camera and Paris would hold it with a dangerously loose grip, tracking me down so she could put the camera in my face and ask me questions. The camera, too big for her to hold with any kind of stability, would wobble violently as Paris searched, and it was difficult to hear anything over the puppy-like breathing coming from behind the lens. I liken this style of cinematography to that of shows like *Storm Chasers* or *Ghost Hunters* or any of the other shows oriented around that kind of real-time thrill.

After a few moments of foraging around the house, she always found me.

"This is my baby brother, Jet. He's playing with his toys now. That's his favorite one right there. Brother, tell them about your toy."

In many of the pictures we have together, even our most recent ones, you can see Paris holds me so tight it almost appears as though she's suffocating me. She tends to smush my cheeks together with one hand while she bites down on her bottom lip—one of her signature idiosyncrasies—which she does whenever she sees something so cute, usually a dog or a small child, she can barely process it. She's done this since she was about four years old.

Even at a very young age, Paris was never a particularly good student. The culture of school did not align with her personality, the dissonance manifesting in a way that felt like rejection to her. She often felt that she didn't fit in with her classmates and that her teachers were working against her, and the inability to identify her role as a young woman and as a student created a great deal of discomfort and sadness within her. The older she got, the more obvious this became to my family. I can admit now that I did not help with all of this because I was at a time in my life where I had no real perception of how my behavior impacted others, and at times, I used my own internal struggle to goad the pain that Paris herself had been enduring.

Not happy with the school in our hometown, Paris found herself a high school across the country in Northern California that she had heard about at a boarding school fair. She applied without telling either of our parents, and upon admittance, she did not approach them beseechingly but rather informed our family that she would be going to California to start school in the fall. She also informed us she had already sorted out financial aid, room and board, and all other primary concerns. This is as "Paris" as it gets when it comes to behavior—she did the same thing when it came to getting a dog, a tattoo, and trip arrangements out of the country. She lived by the law of "don't ask for permission, ask for forgiveness."

While away at school, to our family's relief, she found herself acclimating much better; she began making friends rather quickly and became the star of the volleyball team. This new warmth in her life allowed her to open up to both herself and to others, and thus began her discovery of her true self. She found serenity in knowing there was no one out there to tell her otherwise. However, she also felt guilty being so far from my mom, a guilt that could only hold out for so long—two years to be exact—before she returned home to complete her final year at Highland Park. This way, she could still help run my mother's business and give my mom the care that she now needed more of again.

Paris, a senior, and I, a sophomore at the time, sat next to each other in the first and last class that we ever shared together— AP Psychology. Weirdly, I can't remember whether or not we did our homework together, but I do remember studying with her, both of us quizzing each other, and telling her that maybe if she came to class more, she would understand the material better. My theory failed because she still did better on the tests than I did.

At school, they encouraged her to behave and think like a kid and a student, but at home she had already become a highly functioning woman, albeit a young woman who had also already been harboring a great deal of pain. Once home again, she had become depressed, which I didn't know much about at the time other than noticing that she liked to lay in bed all day. I constantly tried to get her to come outside for a walk or go to the lake but was often met with refusal. I couldn't understand why she would choose to be in bed all day, and she tried with great frustration to explain that it wasn't a choice.

Paris was not born with the hypersensitivity I seemed to have. She was "strong like bull," as my mom would jokingly say. She had a high pain tolerance and didn't mind things like throwing up, the nauseating thrill of roller coasters, getting high, or enduring a bad injury. I, on the other hand, cried when I threw up, winced at pain, and feared the height of roller coasters. Because of this, I think it was also easier for Paris to stuff the emotions she experienced, both the good and bad, deep inside of her wherever she could find room for them. Maybe this is what weighed her down to the point that she needed to be in bed all day, but because I feel everything to a great extent, I began to write and perform and talk through everything I felt. I could not hold onto pain for long simply because I did not have the tolerance to, which made it rather easy to forgive people and let go of any trauma that created a sense of burden, dropping these things from my hands like a hot plate.

Maybe this is why I deeply feared the pain that would come from losing my mom and why I felt I needed to detach from her emotionally, although this form of detachment proved to be infeasible as I watched her health depreciate, whereas Paris only moved deeper into the rough and dark waters of grief. Paris was always a stronger swimmer.

Paris only spent more time with my mom, did more for her, drove three hours from her university every day to care for my mom at a friend's house whom she was briefly staying with while trying to find healing in Los Angeles. I could not bear to watch at the end of my mom's life, but Paris could not bear to feel that she left my mother uncared for.

My mom told Paris many times what to do in the event of her passing away and the expectations she had in regard to both her and me. Paris would dismiss these conversations as best she could because talking about it turned her fear into a deeply painful simulation of reality, but it was clear that Paris had been internalizing my mother's every request.

One of my mother's requests was that we pray for her, constantly. She'd ask the three of us sit by each other, holding hands, and pray to any source higher than ourselves that she would make it out on the other end of this ruthless round of her battle with cancer just as strong as she was before. Paris and I acquiesced uncomfortably.

My mother's relationship to God, whoever He or She was to her, was both evident and complicated. She called herself a "Jew for Jesus," which I thought was funny and directly akin to who she was at heart, but her nebulous relationship to religion made mine feel complex and unmoored while I grew up.

For a large chunk of my life, I believed my mother was raised Catholic because she didn't identify with Jewish culture at all and she told me her family was every ethnicity one can imagine. One day her father was Irish and the next he was technically Argentinian. Her mother was Spanish or African or Scottish, and I could not keep up with the derivatives of our cultural and religious background. All I knew was my last name had Portuguese origins. Therefore, I assumed the existence of my Portuguese blood. My mother and her siblings looked Latin American, so I accepted that as proof. The truth is they were Jewish kids bred from Arizonian parents and Chicagoan grandparents. Yet my mother identified with the Latin American culture; she bought candles with the face of Christ and a variety of saints depicted on the glass encasing, often making homemade enchiladas and tamales. I bought in, ostensibly, and started learning Spanish at a young age to connect with my newfound roots.

Between the Christ candles in my mom's house and the yarmulkes that sat next to the refrigerator in my father's house, ready to be worn at a moment's notice—just in case the occasion called for it, or maybe as an emblem of Jewish appreciation—one might see how my religious beliefs were complicated to the extent of being nonexistent.

I simply gave up trying to understand. All I knew growing up was that there was a God and that He was, I hoped, merciful.

CHAPTER 5

MAZEL TOV, KID

———

Growing up, like many boys, my God was an athlete. His holy religion was sports, and I was a divine worshipper, a dedicated follower—often by way of carpooling.

I found wholehearted contentment in going from one practice to the next, not worrying about anything other than trying to compete at my highest level and washing my face after practice so I wouldn't get acne. My mother, however, did not share my same sentiments about this. I couldn't wrap my mind around why she wasn't content with her son just being an "athlete."

Even though she recognized my abilities from a young age, she didn't choose or care to groom me to be some kind of stellar athlete. She never expressed any kind of desire for me to play sports at the collegiate level, and she was not the mother who came and yelled at my games. In fact, she didn't watch one of my full football games the entire four years I played in high school. I didn't mind that she wasn't there, it was of no real offense to me. I knew she didn't find the game exciting other than when it directly involved her son, and she knew she would hear about it afterward from me or another parent or on social media. I also knew that she had a hard time coming to watch games without wanting to provide ambiguous and abstract pointers afterward.

In the days when she came to watch my basketball games, when the game was over, she would almost always say to me:

"You were great, honey! I just think you need to let it all out there more."

"Ma. What do you mean 'let it all out there'?" I'd ask, confounded and frustrated.

"You know... you need to just let it all out and let yourself go! I think you're too worried."

"Worried about what?"

"I don't know, you tell me. Maybe you get nervous when I come to the games. Maybe I shouldn't come anymore. You always got nervous when I'd watch you play as a kid. You could never shoot the ball when I was watching," she'd say as though grounded in science.

I had heard this theory a hundred times.

"I don't get nervous with you watching. And I'm not worried about anything!" I'd say with significantly more frustration.

"Well, that's not what it looks like! Don't get angry with me, I'm just telling you what I saw. You played really great, and you jump higher than the other kids, but…you know…you just need to work on letting it all out."

This is when I'd give in. Otherwise, we'd go on for another twenty minutes.

"Okay, ma. Got it. I'll be sure to let it all out next time."

My father, however, had taken on a rather enthusiastic attitude toward the future of my football career. He liked the idea of his son being a college football player, especially if it was at a prestigious institution. My father and I are alike that way. We were born as creatures who like an audience and, as all performers seek to do, give that audience something they can "ooh" and "ahh" at. We go for the glory, and although neither he nor I have ever been braggarts, we do like to see the look in others' eyes when we behave impressively. For my father, it would be substantially impressive that his son not only possessed an athletic prowess worthy of collegiate recognition but that it would go so far as to earn his son a rank within the Ivy Leagues. He'd be able to explain this to others should the subject come up. He would be met with responses like, "Wow, that's incredible!" or "Wow, you must have done something right!". And that would be enough for him. Such was the same for myself; I dreamed not so much of the realization of this fantasy but of others' responses to it. My mom, however, did not care for either.

My mother did not care for what the people of the town thought or believed in. Most people don't take on this kind of attitude until they are in their late stages of life, such as grandparents who blatantly disregard what others think about them or their actions. They have surrendered to the natural lack of control over how others perceive them, of pleasing others, and of being likable. Like the older gentleman who farts in a yoga class without embarrassment and understands that it's just natural for him, he does not subscribe to the idea of suppressing his own nature for the sake of others. There is a rather ruthless impenitence that comes with age. It is certainly enviable to an extent. I can see it in my great-grandmother, my mom's grandma, who I visit at her assisted living home a few towns over whenever I am back home from school. I liken her home to a bigger, more fun, more experienced college dorm room. It's full of her contemporaries, some of whom she meets with daily to eat or play cards. The facility also offers all kinds of activities and lectures which, when I'm there, I attend wearily with her.

It is often not until I spend time with the unapologetic and the unconcerned, such as my great grandma, that I realize just how apologetic and concerned I am.

The last time I was there, we watched a lecture on the different kinds of flutes. The man delivering the lecture was in his sixties and greeted some of the crowd by name; it was apparent he had been there before.

"Nice to see you again, Mel," he said to a man in the front row.

Finding another familiar face, he smiled and said, "That's a great shirt, Sandy."

He worked the room with an air of popularity. It was like I was watching the cool kid walk into the school lunchroom.

A cool kid giving a lecture on flutes—how cliché! My grand-mother and I sat in the back, and she fell asleep not long after he began sermonizing on piccolos.

When we eat together, she does not particularly use what most would refer to as common courtesy; there is no "please" or 'thank you" or coyness about changing an order or asking for extra ketchup. If we are at a restaurant, when the waiter approaches there is no "hello" or "how are you?" She'll just burst through the greeting with her order. "Yeah I'll have two eggs with chicken sausage and on the side. I'd like two English muffins with butter and strawberry jelly."

The server usually won't even have their notepad out yet because they didn't anticipate the readiness with which she would accost them, but they figure it out, otherwise she has no problem telling them that they have not.

My mother was not too dissimilar. She did not care for small talk or whether the server liked her or not, and she was not afraid to have something sent back to the kitchen. This was always a monumental and tragically embarrassing moment for Paris and me.

"Yeah, can you tell the chef this is too garlic-y. I'm a chef and I can taste that the garlic is overdone," she'd say.

God forbid we should receive a piece of fish that was "too fishy" —that was the quickest way for a server to learn that our mother, in fact, was a chef and the fish, in fact, was much too fishy.

We never knew why she would add that she was a chef, but she did this often, attaching some kind of occupational title to the remark she was making.

"I'm a doctor and–" or "I'm an author and –."

I think, however, she would just say it whenever she felt she needed validity for whatever that remark may be. Paris and I would give her grief about this tendency with harmless teasing and jokes.

"I'm a zoologist and I say these tigers don't have enough space to roam damnit! Oh, and they're inflamed, so you're going to need to take them off all dairy products!"

"Oh, shut up! You kids are always so embarrassed by everything," She'd say before giving into the laughter.

She didn't mind laughing at herself and would often remind me that if you can't laugh at yourself, then you shouldn't be allowed to laugh at anyone else.

She would pitch jokes about herself to me, like the Orbit gum skit, and insisted:

"You have to tell this when you're on SNL."

That was one of her infamous eccentricities—making declarations rather than hypotheticals. It was never "if" you are on SNL or "if" you go to this or that university or "if" you are successful, it was "when." It wasn't like she said it as some profound manifesto, but simply as though it were reality.

For a moment, sensing the unflinching conviction in her voice, you felt absolutely certainty of its truth. One thing was for sure, if I did eventually ever want to make it onto Saturday Night Live, I would need better jokes than the ones she was offering up.

"You should write a skit about how your mother always sent food back to the kitchen and would tell the restaurant that she was a chef and then they'd ask her to actually come back to the kitchen to make her own meal for herself. And then you could show, or 'cut to,' five hours later and I'd be running the kitchen and then at the end of the night, so many hours later, I'd return to the dinner table and say, 'Where were we?' and then the skit would end right there."

Her laugh moved her at her core but only for a few seconds until she would revisit the idea with some further detail:

"And the title of the sketch would be 'The Chef.'"

Yeah, she was never great with titles either, although she was known to claim her excellence just about anywhere, whether it be as a world-class water skier or an exceptional tennis player. She reminded me often that I got my athletic genes from her, and she liked to compete with me when I was younger to prove it.

"Make no mistake, I may be your mom, but I can still whoop your ass," she'd say while we walked onto the tennis courts.

And yet she still did not care for my career in athletics. She, instead, was adamant about getting me involved with activities like ballet or hip-hop classes. She was most persistent about getting me into theatre, but that was only one of what seemed like hundreds of things. I would combat her maternal force on all of them—the discomfort I had with the idea of doing anything but sports intense and unconquerable—but she didn't care whether or not I was comfortable. She did not buckle under my howling whines and complaints.

"Jet, when are you going to stop fighting me on these things and just accept that I know what's best for you? I don't care what you say, you're going to that ballet class!"

I had no choice, and, subsequently, I harbored a fleeting resentment for her because of it. On the day I had to go to ballet class, I wore my hood up so no one could see me, and I prayed to a God I didn't even believe in at the time that I wouldn't see anyone I knew. I showed up to the studio in my basketball shorts and a cutoff to exude as much masculinity as I could. My hands were sweating, and I avoided looking anyone in the eye as I walked in. I was twelve years old and at the very worst time in my life for this. The class was comprised of about twenty female students and me. As if out of a movie, the teacher, an austere and sinewy blonde woman, called for the room's attention.

"Class we have a new student with us today. This is Jet."

I considered making a run for it, but instead just stood there in all of my prepubescent glory, smiling nervously and hoping they wouldn't hear my heart beating through my tank top. Some of the girls laughed while others smirked knowingly. They were in their element, and I was not. I felt like live chum in the water. What I felt at the time was that attending a ballet class would surely pervade global news; all of my friends would hear about it and I would be laughed at for years to come. I wanted to follow up the teacher's announcement with an assurance to everyone that my mother had made me come. This was not my choice, and that, you see, my mom is crazy, and her insanity was the reason for my enrollment. Hopefully, they would find understanding in their hearts. They would forgive my attendance because it was the consequence of a merciless parent.

I stuck it out through the entire class, but it quickly became one of the most painful and subsisting hours of my adolescent years. An endless hour spent in basketball shorts, a cutoff t-shirt, and ballet slippers. Looking back on it now, this is one of my favorite and most entertaining memories. I couldn't know at the time how this would build character.

When it was over, I pleaded with my mom and told her I would do anything it took to never return to the class. She succumbed but not without a fair trade.

"Fine, but then you're coming to dahn yoga with me this weekend."

"Mom, please. No!"

"Jet, it's one or the other."

I knew she was not bluffing. My mother did not bend or leave us choices that she did not want to leave. She was not strict about us partying or hanging out with friends, but when it came down to what she wanted for us, she did not budge. If you argued too much, there were consequences, which my sister and I both learned quickly.

So that next weekend I went with her to a dahn yoga class, which is essentially a mix of yoga, tai chi, and martial arts exercises. I had decided I would go and, instead following the instruction of the teacher, I would use the class to stretch for an hour. However, once the class began and I was not following along with the exercises, my mom looked at me with a piercing glare that articulated, frighteningly clear, "Fall in line or I'll beat you right here in front of these people." I could feel the stress relief already!

I reluctantly and stiffly moved through the motions of class, searching the room desperately for a clock to gauge how much longer I had left. No luck. I guess time was of no importance to these people who purged themselves of worry and conflict through intense and loud breathing, who swung their arms and hit themselves up and down their bodies.

Meanwhile, the only release I was hoping for was the release of students back into the world, free of intermittent gongs and the soft matted floors and away from the dim light of the studio. As soon as we got out, I would be able to give my mom grief for lying about the class being only an hour long, when it was actually an hour and a half.

Before the class ended, the "master" had us all sit down in a traditional meditation pose and create a ball of energy between our hands. He told us to work with and move it around like we were playing with an elastic ball. With my eyes closed, I put my hands out and just went through the motions. I didn't feel a single atom of this energy he spoke of. After the energy ball session was over, we bowed and said, "Namaste," and I was out of the room before the master could even finish saying, "Have a great rest of the weekend." I was like a kid being let out for recess.

I thought this class would be no different from all other classes my mother had forced me into in the sense that I would go to one class and then make an excuse for why it was a waste of money or time. I had to formulate my argument, so it was oriented around her benefit rather than mine. When she told me a week later that we were going back to dahn yoga, I told her I didn't think I should go because I would only distract her, minimizing the value and impact of the class. I was giving her cold, hard science. I told her I would instead practice from home now that I had been to a class and seen the exercises and hone my skills in private before spending the money to go back to another class.

"Nice try, Jet. You're coming. Get dressed and let's go."

Oh man, the amount of times I had heard, "Get dressed and let's go."

That meant, "You have no say in the matter, now either you get dressed for what we're about to do or I take you as you are now."

There was one day while enrolled in a summer math camp before entering the fifth grade where I was particularly exhausted and did not want to go to the camp. After I had blatantly disregarded my mother's first, more gentle alarm, she came back into the room with the heavier threat.

"Jet, get dressed and let's go. I'm not going to say it again."

Still, I closed my eyes thinking she would give in and let her baby boy get the rest he needed. Not quite. What she did, however, was lift me out of bed once I had fallen asleep again and put me in the backseat of the car. I woke up to her saying, "Jet, we're here. You're already late so hurry in."

We were at the front of the school and I had no shirt or pants on. I was just wearing the boxer-briefs and socks I had slept in.

"Get dressed and go, Jet. You're late and I have to be some-where in twenty minutes!"

I threw on the uniform she had put on the seat next to me, but there were no belt or shoes.

"Mom, I can't go in. I don't have shoes! Or my belt! I'm not going in like this."

"That's too bad, Jet. You should have gotten ready when I told you to and this wouldn't have happened."

Frustrated and nervous to go inside, I walked into my school shoeless and having to pull my pants up every ten steps or so. Needless to say, I never slept in again that summer.

Years later, I was either going to be dragged to this class in jeans and a t-shirt, which would be problematic and ridiculous considering it's a movement-oriented class, or I could accept my fate and put on more appropriate clothes. I took a second to decide, and my mother was apparently listening to the stillness in my room after she walked out and knew I was not changing.

"Jet, you think I'm fucking around but I'm not. You better be getting dressed!" I got dressed.

What I hoped would be a onetime occurrence soon became regular, reluctance attendance of dahn yoga classes. Soon, I was pushed into the meditation classes at the same studio, and after it was their tai chi class, which I thought would actually be cool because maybe we'd learn how to knock people over by using wind and energy forces. I found out both of those ideas, each to their own degree, were and were not the art of tai chi. The movements we did during class were how I envisioned them to be, but I didn't see anyone in my energy path stumbling from my actions. I was only moderately disappointed, however.

During these classes, I would watch my mother perform the exercises like a woman possessed. This studio was her church and her synagogue. My mom would go wild in these classes. She would breathe heavily and "let it all out," and even though others in the class were behaving similarly, I felt deeply embarrassed of my mother, how loud she was, and what a scene she seemed to be making. Sometimes she would start crying and the teacher would say:

"That's right, let it all out!"

Everyone seemed to be "letting it all out" but me, and I couldn't be certain about what this "it" they were referring to was exactly but, evidently, "it" was very strong and very painful. I realized later that what they were referring to was the same "it" I had learned about from my mother several years prior. I would stand there watching the others, stiff with the tension of my own resistance to surrendering, and all I wanted was to leave.

After class, my mom would explain how much "stuff" she was holding onto, how amazing that class was for her, and how much she needed it. She didn't realize she was still holding onto certain memories, carrying it on her shoulders like heavy, sharp rocks that left her bleeding and infected— the wounds of the past. This was the "it" that she was working with such ferocity to "let out."

My mother grew up in what she called a "fucked-up family." She was the middle child between a younger sister and older brother. She became the oldest when my uncle, who was also my mother's closest friend, passed away from a drug overdose.

I remember being in the living room watching television with my family and our home phone rang. I don't know who called, but my mother got up to answer it. The phone was just beside the tv, and a few moments later, she broke down crying hysterically. My father hurried over from the couch to where my mother was crouched, holding only onto the wire of the phone as it dangled out of her hand. She held the wire close as though it were her child. She did not let go of the wire even as my father grabbed onto her for an embrace. Somehow, it seemed like my father already knew. Meanwhile, Paris and I, for those first few minutes of grieving, were completely lost.

When they finally told us Uncle Bradley had passed away, I didn't know what to feel. I was sad but only because my mother was so deeply sad, a sorrow not quite of my own accord. I had only spent what seemed a very small amount of time with him. He was an artist living in Arizona, famous for his beadwork, and often flew all over the world to showcase his work and meet with high-profile buyers. He was tan and sinewy with long beautiful hair and dark eyes. He looked like a Spanish rendition of Jesus.

When my sister and I asked how he died, our parents told us that he was hit by a truck. In my mind, I envisioned one of those big cement trucks with the rollers on the back of it, the roller falling off the back of the truck and wildly off the road, crushing him under its weight. Maybe it happened while he was getting his picture taken, or maybe he was on the phone with a friend. Either way, he must have not seen it coming. That is how I believed he died for many years. It wasn't until I got older that my mom told me about the way he had used drugs.

He had been bullied growing up because of his sexuality, and my mother assumed the responsibility of protecting him. He was a fragile artist with parents who deprived him of the love and support every child inherently needs. Instead, my mother was there to give him love. They went to class together, shopped together, told hushed late-night stories to one another, and even shared clothes.

My father likes telling the story of the time he bought my mother a blouse for her birthday and how at dinner later that week Bradley showed up wearing that very blouse. My father would follow the story with the clever yet honest admittance that the blouse looked better on Bradley than on my mother.

A week after my uncle's passing, we flew out to San Diego as a family and took a small boat out to scatter his ashes in the ocean. Neither of his parents were there. I could not fathom the idea of my own parents not showing up for something like this, how such a thing would bring me pain even in the afterlife.

My grandfather, as I'm told, would beat his children with a belt when they behaved poorly, and his wife, their mother, did not care at all. She was not around, and her kids were left to take care of themselves. This is how my mother became the caretaker of the family, the one who cooked and cleaned and made sure her sister and brother were well kept.

The source of my mother's pain and trauma was rather obvious. She told Paris and I stories of her childhood that made me sick to my stomach and stirred within me a pity that I wished to eradicate. She worked through this pain with yoga, qigong, and other eastern practices, but there were a handful of things that she had been unable to successfully work through.

This is where life had taken her. She had kids of her own who she cared so deeply for it sometimes brought pain to her heart—seeing that the heart cannot fully know its deepest love without also knowing its deepest pain—and her desire for her son to have the best brought us to dahn yoga classes together.

Years later, after a long hiatus from these classes, my mother told me I needed a private lesson with Master Adahae—the man who ran the yoga studio—because, so she said, I had to work through my own trauma. I assured my mother I didn't have any trauma I had to work through. She and I both knew this was not true.

"Of course you do, Jet. You've had to put up with a crazy mother who has cancer," she said only half-jokingly.

I went because, as you know, I really had no option.

Master Adahae and I sat in a smaller, private studio just outside of the classroom studio, the floor soft and light greenish-yellow and the walls decorated with Japanese scrolls—some with characters and others with birds or flowers. He sat across from me cross-legged with perfect posture, almost unblinking, a shorter white man with a groomed black beard and garments that I imagined a monk would wear to work out. He took a deep breath before he asked in a soft, clear voice, almost like he was singing:

"So, what's going on with you?"

"Well, I'm going to be a senior in high school next year… so that's exciting. I'm pretty sure I'm going to play football at Yale or Georgetown."

"That *is* exciting."

The names of those schools did not affect him in the slightest. He did not respond to my ego.

I wanted to tell him about all of the things that had been keeping me up at night, the things that pressed on my mind and inculcated my blood with fear. I feared for the life of my mother and my father, often anticipating the worst.

What if I didn't get into any college, and did not live up to who I thought I was? What if both of my parents died? What would I do to provide for myself and my family? Would my youth dissipate as the responsibilities began to rain down on me? I could feel all of my insecurities and worries beginning to build up. I wanted to let go of the Jet who felt he needed to lift weights to build an egoic suit of armor and the Jet who had to make jokes to entertain and distract. I had only been in the room for five minutes. He had only asked a very simple question, but there was something about his energy, which now surrounded the both of us in this small studio, that made me feel as though I might cry.

"Yeah, I guess. I'm not really sure where I'm gonna wind up and the uncertainty of all of it scares the shit out of me—excuse my language. I also fear for my mom when I go to college. I just don't want anything bad to happen to my family. The thought of losing my parents scares me. My dad had a heart attack this year and I thought we lost him. I don't know what I would've done."

Master Adahae just sat there and listened. He listened not just with his ears, but with his eyes and his heart; he heard what I was telling him with his full body.

Meanwhile, I could hardly focus on, nonetheless absorb, what he was telling me. I was too distracted by the feeling that my throat was beginning to split wide open. There was so much I wanted to say next, but this was not a conversational therapy session. His breath moved in and out easily. I could see his chest and stomach rise and sink as he breathed, evoking visualizations of his breath that helped me breathe easier.

He had me begin the meditation flat on my back as he did, inhaling and exhaling deeply. He told me to focus on my own breath, to envision I was breathing in white light and it was beginning to circulate around my mind and body like air particles. He told me when I exhaled, I should envision breathing out all of the things I feared and anything else that was distracting me from the present moment. After a few moments, he fell silent and I continued breathing, my eyes closed while I did my best to focus on my breath.

Without seeing it coming, I had fallen asleep and into a dream that I was in a football game. I was playing well and on one of the plays, I caught the ball and began running, the open field ahead of me and only the end zone in sight, and I could feel excitement growing as I ran toward the impending celebration. I was approaching now, running faster than before, but about thirty yards away from the end zone I was tackled from behind with the force of a small sedan. My body jolted and I awoke in a panic.

Master Adahae was sitting in the same position, just breathing.

"What happened?" he asked, unshakably calm.

I told him the dream.

He asked me to move into the same posture he was holding, the traditional meditative, cross-legged pose that always badly hurt my knees and back. He asked me to return to my breathing. Closing my eyes and breathing deeply again, I cooled off from the heat my body had worked up during the dream. After about five minutes, he asked me to place my hands in front of me, leaving some distance between the two, and feel the ball of energy between them. I followed his instruction, but this time there was something there. In all of the other classes I had just put my hands up and moved them around, pretending I was cradling something, but now there was something tangible between them.

"Move the ball around. Feel it move and stretch like elastic in your hands."

I began familiarizing the ball, which felt as real as any of my soccer balls at home, except this one was magnetic. After a few moments of this, the ball felt so real I got freaked out and opened my eyes because I believed he had placed an object in my hands as some kind of metaphoric demonstration of energy. I opened my eyes, but there was nothing there. He sat in the same position across from me, breathing deeply and noticing I had opened my eyes.

"Sorry. I uh—I just thought you put something there...it's just all the times I've done this before I've never felt anything, but just now, I felt it. I felt it like it was a real ball."

I smiled as I told him. I felt invigorated by something fresh, although I did not know what. It was like feeling hydrated after being deprived of water, not realizing I was parched until that first sip. This was the first time I felt the energy of The Universe, and it was right there between my hands. The session ended shortly after and I left the studio with the sensation that I had just woken up from a long, deep sleep.

I had never been given a bar mitzvah, but I consider this moment my bar mitzvah. My crossing over from a diluted world of ego into a world of brilliant clarity.

As soon as I got home, I told my mom I needed to set up another appointment.

CHAPTER 6

IVY LEAGUE EGO

———

Like all bar mitzvahs, even though the boy becomes recognized by the community as a young man, he is still, very
much so, an inexperienced youth searching for meaning, for
his "place" as they say. He must continue his journey toward
understanding how he relates both to himself and to the rest
of the world.

The bar mitzvah is only the surface, beyond which he must
begin to dig his way to the core of life and his experiences,
finding roots the further inward he goes. Along the way,
somewhere, is the realization that the reason he must dig—
cautious not to cause harm as he does—is so he may know
how to nourish those roots of his. And so, he may understand more fully how what comes of those roots will not only
impact his own life, but the many lives surrounding his. In
this, he will come to find joy.

It was clear after that session with Master Adahae that I had
my digging cut out for me, but I rejoiced in the belief that
there was something beautiful to be found.

After that first jolt of clarity, the meditation and yoga classes I had begun to attend were waking me up, but only in a slow and gradual kind of way. I was still, in more ways than not, asleep and unconscious to the present moment, enveloped in my own ego. The ego, I would come to learn later on, encompasses any and all fear, gossip, complaining, contempt, judgement, envy, insecurity, and anxiety. Amongst other definitions the ego, as Pema Chödrön describes it, is "that which resists what is."[4]

And Eckhart Tolle describes the ego as: "A dysfunctional relationship with the present moment."[5]

Before me, in the Now, my senior year of high school was unfolding, which I was committed to using as a launch pad from which I could depart from the community my ego had come to resent. By this time, I had identified with this idea that I was of greater value than my peers, that I was different or some kind of "chosen one." I identified with thoughts of myself being the kid who would leave his hometown and become legendary. I felt a need to prove to everyone who I really was, although I can now admit that I did not have the slightest clue about that.

The image I had of myself was one I had created to impress upon the public eye, and it was one I presumed was in accordance with my "worth." I would be the Ivy League football player, the scholarship student, and the star athlete at

---

4   Pema Chödrön , *Welcoming the Unwelcome: Wholehearted Living in a Brokenhearted World,* (Boulder: Shambhala, 2019).

5   Eckhart Tolle, *A New Earth: Awakening to Your Life's Purpose,* (London: Penguin, 2016).

Georgetown—no, Yale sounds much better! They'd ask me where I was going in the fall and I'd be able to say I was "off to play football at Yale, oh and please don't write to me but be sure to tell your kids and your grandkids about what I have done here, and about the legacy that I've left!"

The ego comes disguised as many different qualities. At this time, my ego came to my door dressed like ambition, or maybe it was determination. Either way, the costume was convincing enough for me. While the other students were inflicted by "seniorities," the majority already having committed to universities where I was sure they'd remain by each other's side in the same groups and talk about the same things and the same people and eat the same food. I wanted nothing to do with it. I wanted something big and far away to separate myself because I felt I was different. My ego, like the small devil on the shoulder, told me day after day that I did not like these people whom I had grown up around, and that I should harbor bitterness toward them.

Why? Because, as I came to learn later, the biggest challenge for the ego is to be around people who you have known for the longest time—whether it's your parents, siblings, or spouse, or in this case, the kids you've grown up with.[6]

The reason behind this difficulty is because egolessness requires absolute presence, but it is tough to achieve when we share a long history with someone. My history with my friends, directly in conflict with my identifications of who I

---

6   Eckhart Tolle, *A New Earth: Awakening to Your Life's Purpose*, (London: Penguin, 2016).

sought to become, were a great source of distraction stripping me from the Now. It became a challenge to enjoy my remaining time in high school because my ego, belligerent behind the wheel, was driving me into unforeseeable distances.

My ego had created resistance to so many things that, in reality, were not applying any pressure whatsoever on me. The reality was I had great friends at this school, great experiences, people I confided in who supported me through hardship, and families that opened their doors to me time and time again.

What was really happening, on a much deeper level I was completely unconscious of, was I was experiencing my own inner conflict. I was clinging to ideas of who I thought I needed to be, rather than surrendering to the present experience of who I already was. I was letting fear and insecurity dictate the way I related to the world and those around me, rather than leading with love. My constant desire for something more led me, time and time again, into a realm of unconsciousness far from everything I already had to be grateful for in this life that was already before me—my family, friends, teachers, and experiences. I was chasing after something that was already within me like a dog after its own tail. Too stubborn, too distracted, and too lost in the external to bother looking inward for the peace I was seeking.

While everyone was already accepted or receiving their acceptance to universities, I was flying around the country and driving across the state from one football showcase to the next chasing after my own sense of worth.

The New England showcase, which happened at the end of the academic year, hosted nearly all of the schools of my interest, and I was convinced this showcase was the golden ticket into the school of my dreams, the facilitator of my fate. And that is exactly how I proposed the opportunity to my mother. She acquiesced. Boston, here I come!

CHAPTER 7

PROM NIGHT

—

"Wow look at you, Mr. Sinatra! My God, you're so handsome it's sick."

"Thank you, Ma. What do you think of the shoes? Too much?"

I was wearing my dad's tuxedo shoes that were two sizes too big—my dress socks layered over two pairs of basketball socks compensated for the extra room.

"No, I love them! Wait, don't move. Let me take a picture."

I struck a few goofy poses, and she couldn't help but laugh.

"Okay, give me a few real ones."

I straightened myself up and did what she asked. My dad and older brother August—older by nine years, and technically my half-brother because we share the same father but not the same mother—walked in through the front door a few seconds later.

It was my junior year of high school and I had been invited to the prom at a neighboring high school. I was invited by a close friend and was looking forward to the evening, seeing as it was my first prom. I had been eager for the opportunity to wear a black tuxedo ever since I had come to believe that the definition of cool could be summed up in two words: Frank Sinatra.

"Steve, come here and look how handsome our son is."

"Wow! Mr. J.E.T.!"

My dad has done this for as long as I can remember—he spells my name out when addressing me.

"Hey everybody! Come and see how good I look!" August yelled, quoting Will Ferrell from *Anchorman*.[7]

To me, August has always been one of the funniest people I know. His humor is a perfect mix of random absurdity and precise cleverness. Growing up, I only wanted to be like him; he was a great athlete and his friends were big and athletic and made jokes that I couldn't understand at the time but desperately wanted to. I wanted him to be my trainer and coach when I was much younger, but instead he'd offer one-on-one competitions in the driveway or the yard and I'd be left outside crying after losing horribly. He was known to trash talk during all of our games because that was his

7 Adam McKay, *Anchorman: The Legend of Ron Burgundy*, (Glendale, CA: DreamWorks Pictures, 2004. DVD).

style, part of his humor. He'd talk to himself and imaginary referees during the game.

"And one! Ref, he's all over me! Can a kid get a call out here?" he'd say toward the garage as though directed at the officials.

He was ruthless when it came to competitions, and for a long time, I took it as a sign that he didn't like me all that much—that he saw me as nothing more than a measly opponent rather than a younger brother. As I got older, we were able to develop a healthier relationship built on a stronger foundation of understanding for one another. I naturally became my own man, but undoubtedly still held onto some of the features I had adopted from him.

Because of this, I've been known to do a great impression of August. So, when my mother told me to get together with Aug for a picture, she got the idea that this would be a good time for me to do so.

My mom was known to do this frequently. She'd tell me to do an impression for someone who was over or sing or she'd tell me to speak Spanish to someone who was a native Spanish speaker. My Spanish wasn't even at a third-grade level but she would tell them I was fluent. You can imagine how disappointed they were when we began a conversation and I couldn't make it past "Estoy bien, y tú?"

She liked to film me when I performed for her and got very aggravated if I protested her right to record. My mother was known to have a temper, but the chemotherapy, as it is medically admitted to, intensified whatever volatility had already existed within her. This is known to some as "chemo rage." The more treatments she underwent, the more she became like a sour patch kid. One moment she was the sweetest woman you'd ever met, the next she was wrathful. Paris and I could only hope the former overcame the latter.

"Jet, you're going to miss me when I'm gone, and you'll wish you sung for your mother more and weren't so stubborn!"

Now she was requesting an impression of my older brother, her phone ready to document this supposed brilliance.

I delivered a brief, half-assed impression of August, which provoked a laugh from Aug and my father but not from my mother.

Disappointed, she rolled her eyes and said "No, Jet. C'mon show him what you showed me the other day."

I wasn't sure what she was talking about. I couldn't remember doing a bit about my brother for her the other day, which did not bode well for me. Her recollection, or forgetfulness, of details had also been exacerbated by the chemotherapy and newer treatments she had been receiving. Her mind and temper began to falter more so than ever from the strength of her medicine—what is known to the medical community as "chemo brain."

"Ma, what are you talking about?"

"You know what I'm talking about, don't be embarrassed. Just do it."

"Are you talking about the face?"

"No Jet, the impression you do of him. C'mon!"

Now, there was tension in the room, and I was past the threshold of uncomfortable. I could also feel August's discomfort and my dad thinking, "Typical Dena."

"Mom, I don't know what you're talking about. Seriously. Just take the picture and let's go."

She was not dropping it.

"Don't make me seem like I'm crazy, Jet, just do the fucking impression."

I laughed nervously, trying to dismiss this whole thing. "You are crazy mom, c'mon just forget it."

Her face became red with anger, and I could see her tears welling up now. There was nothing my mother despised more than someone making her feel she was crazy, especially when that someone was her own blood.

We had learned to not interject with any kind of correction or rebuttal when my mother was talking to someone else because of how it made her look. She internalized it as her own child shaming her. It was, simply put, treasonous.

I could see she felt betrayal more now than ever before. I feared for myself, but I had dug this hole and, even though

I desperately wanted to climb out, I knew I would be buried in it.

August tried calming my mother down by telling her everything was fine, but it was too late.

"Mom, just drop it. Please."

My mother exploded. She threw her phone and came at me, yelling and sobbing and punching me harder than she had ever hit me before. She hit my face and chest and grabbed onto me with the grip that left bloody nail marks many times before.

This was not my mother. This was the burning manifestation of all her pain she had collected from over the years. She came at me with vengeance for the men in her life who had abused her—her father and her ex-boyfriend.

My dad had to pull her off of me and August stood there horrified.

"Don't fucking come home! Go live with your father!"

"Dena, that's enough," my dad said calmly, firmly.

It was seldom my father raised his voice, but instead, he'd speak with an austerity that made you stiffen. His sternness, because so infrequently taken on, evoked in Paris and me, and even our mother, a freezing cold remorse.

Now my father, August, and I got into my dad's car and I did my best to hold it together, but to no avail.

I was embarrassed for my mother and scared of what she was becoming. I was embarrassed for myself because this unfolded in front of August and I cried in front of him.

"I just feel bad you guys had to see that," I said through the tears now staining my fresh tuxedo jacket. Doing my best to wipe them off of, I realized my mother had also ripped my shirt.

We made a quick stop at August's mom's nearby house where he grabbed a clean white shirt and a belt for me to wear. I changed in the driveway, still trembling from adrenaline.

I could feel the notifications coming in rapidly on my phone, buzzing like a small earthquake from furious texts that my mother was sending. Among these messages were also messages from a few of my friends who were already at the house for prom pictures.

"Where you at bro? We're leaving soon."

I did my best to collect myself, putting on my best smile for all the pictures. Needless to say, I didn't have much fun at prom because I had been replaying the scene over and over again in my mind.

I had to shut my phone off until I was ready to call my dad to pick me up from the after party.

I slept at my dad's the next two nights, but when school came around on Monday, I didn't have any clothes to wear because my entire closet was at my mom's. I was too afraid of going back there, so I wore my father's clothes to school that Monday. However, he and I are vastly different sizes, so the satirically oversized outfit I wore to school that day lent me the aesthetic of an early 2000s rapper.

"Jet what's good with the outfit, you steal those pants from your dad?" my friend Jack quipped.

I spit back as slick as I could, "Good call bro. My dumbass slept at his house and forgot all my clothes. This is the new look."

"I'm with it!" he said, still joking.

After school, I came to the conclusion I had no choice but to go back to my mom's house to grab some clothes.

I stopped at my dad's to grab a suitcase before heading home, praying my mother wouldn't be there. But, of course, she was.

My heart was beating heavily before I could even get out of my car. I went in through the side door and ran up the stairs to my room, starting to unpack my drawers and throw them into the suitcase as quick as I could.

I heard my mother's footsteps ascending the stairs, and moments later, she was at my door watching me pack.

"So, you're just going to leave me? After everything I've done for you, for you to treat me like that in front of your father and your brother is fucking sickening."

"Mom, you told me to move in with dad. I'm sorry. I didn't mean to get you worked up like that."

"Yes, you did."

"I didn't. Why would I do that?"

"Because you fucking get off on it. You want to make it seem like I'm some crazy mom when your dad already thinks I'm crazy. He and I were talking about getting back together. You think that's going to happen now after he saw that?"

"I'm sorry," I said quietly.

I didn't know what else to say; I felt cornered, the lump in my throat now preventing me from speaking.

"For you to do that to your own mother," she was crying now. "That's the fucking thanks I get for doing everything for you? I cook and clean and work for you, and I feed you and make sure you do whatever the fuck you want to do all the fucking time! I make it so your life is perfect.

Oh, big fucking deal you have to take me to my treatments every once in a while or drop off food for my clients! You don't do shit and I asked you to do one thing. One. Simple. Thing. Just do a stupid fucking impression, but you can't even do that!"

"Mom, enough!" I tried to channel my father's sternness.

It backfired.

As soon as I raised my voice, she lost it. I stood there with my head down while she beat down on me with all the strength she had left. I tried to restrain her with a hug, but she shoved me even harder. I needed to escape, but she was in the doorway and I had to get the suitcase.

Even in that moment, I knew it was not me who she was beating. She was beating Tim who had sent her home with bruises before.

I grabbed my suitcase and dodged my mother as best as I could, running out of the house and into my car. She ran out in the driveway, following me, and I quickly locked my doors, prompting her to pull at them—I felt I was living a nightmare or acting in some kind of bizarre horror film. I pulled my car out of the driveway as quick as I ever had, almost running over her feet, and sped off in the direction of my dad's house.

Sitting in my Spanish class the next day, the school's security officer Boscoe interrupted with a knock on the door.

"Hi, I just need to see Jet," he told my teacher.

The class looked at me. I got up and began to walk over, but Boscoe stopped me.

"I would take your stuff with you," he said.

I packed up and walked out, flashing my teacher a weak, forced smile.

"Your mom is here," Boscoe told me once we got into the hall.

Oh god.

She was in the principal's office waiting. She offered an apologetic, ashamed smile as I approached as though I were the one reclaiming her from trouble with the school principal. She thanked Boscoe, grabbed my arm gently like I was her son again, and we walked out together.

"I forgot what the inside of this school looked like," she said, trying to make a joke.

I smiled softly only because I didn't want the students passing by to think anything was wrong. *Everything's cool, I'm cool. Nothing to see here.*

We got into her car and, after a few moments of silence, she began to cry.

"Jet, I feel so bad about what I did. I mean really, I'm sick over it. You know I love you more than anything in this world. I mean I love you and your sister so much that it kills me. Really. You know I don't like when you make me seem crazy. I mean I know I'm crazy, but I don't want to feel anymore crazy than I actually am. And you know the medicine from these treatments fuck me all up."

"I know, ma. It's okay. I shouldn't have done that to you. I'm sorry."

She looked at my arm and saw it was all scratched up.

"Did I do that to you?"

I didn't say anything, but she knew the answer.

"My poor baby. I'm so sorry."

She grabbed my arm and kissed it as though it would heal from her kiss.

I couldn't know whether it would or not, but either way I forgave her as I always had.

I forgave her as I still do.

CHAPTER 8

THE RIGHT WRONG TURN

———

There was a palpable heaviness during the weekend trip to the New England showcase. The pressure of what I felt I needed to accomplish that weekend—a force I had created for myself through my relentless inner dialogue about how important this weekend was—was quickly becoming a source of self-injury. As if my stomach wasn't tightly wound up enough, my mom was not feeling at her best that weekend and experienced intense pain in her arms and chest. I began to consider the possibility I wouldn't even make it to the showcase and would have to rush my mother to a local hospital where she would need emergency surgery.

Thankfully I did not, but I asked her every thirty minutes or so how she was feeling. She took some medicine to alleviate the pain and assured me she would be fine, finding a seat for herself in the bleachers to watch her son play for admittance into the school of his dreams. Out on the field now in front of hundreds of coaches and other competitors, I felt I was performing not just for my future but for my mother's well-being. I thought by winning I could, by some kind of bizarre miracle, heal her. I could give her a reason to celebrate and we could both go home, riding on the pleasant comfort that this trip was well worth all the trouble of travel and hotel expenses. On the other hand, I feared having to deal with the consequential guilt of feeling I had wasted our time and money by coming all this way. I'm aware of the aphorism "pressure makes diamonds," and while I'm sure it may be true in theory, I did not serve as proof of that sentiment.

I performed terribly throughout the three days of competition, growing more frustrated with myself throughout the course of the showcase. While I talked to some coaches, I was not garnering interest from the schools I really wanted. Many of the coaches told me I needed to get my ACT score up—something that had been a source of confidence for me going into the camp, but was quickly obliterated and remolded into a source of insecurity.

I left Boston feeling defeated, almost ashamed, but my mom told me not to beat myself up over it.

"It wasn't meant to be," she said, as she always did when something didn't work out.

She was a resolute proponent of the notion that if something were meant to be—which is also to say "destined to be"—then it would work itself out. She believed in the perfect order and reasoning of The Universe. I, however, had a hard time believing in this, let alone finding comfort in its ethereal truth.

So I kept pushing. I would force my way into these dreams if that's what it took. If only I knew then that mother always knows best.

Now, because the showcase didn't go the way I fantasized it would, I would have to improvise a new way into the esteemed universities I so desperately wanted to attend. I knew a good amount of kids who had gone out to preparatory boarding schools and kids who had done what was called a postgraduate, or "PG," year. A PG year was a fifth year of high school that was really meant for athletes to increase their chances of being recruited by a college. What was perfect about this is most of the kids who go out east for a PG year usually do so to gain admittance into an Ivy League or NESCAC school—schools of high merit and honorable legacy.

From a young age, I've noticed within me a strange imbalance when it comes to these kinds of moral dilemmas. The choice of freedom, which always comes from a place deeper than all else, or the choice of esteem and glorified character were my options.

I'm reminded of this every time I watch a movie like *Dead Poets Society* or *School Ties*. The imbalance comes from my rather untraceable affinity for the idea of getting dressed up nicely, hair combed, sporting neatly buttoned shirts with tightly knotted ties and tending tirelessly to an arduous academic schedule at a school that requires of me the most steadfast demonstration of dignity, discipline, and rigor.

I couldn't decide whether I cherished this kind of environment because I seemed to thrive when people expected things of me—when there were high standards to be met—or because of my propensity to break rules and defy authority. There is a greater deal of room for rules to be broken in a stringent environment than one with few to no rules or standards at all. At a preparatory school, I could count on the inevitable impulse to sneak out of dorm rooms and stand up to teachers who I did not agree with, and I could certainly, as I saw it, depend on the urge to stand upon desks yelling, "O' Captain my captain!"[8] There would be room for subversion, bringing unexpected life to the otherwise lifeless, and to fall out of line, which would garner the attention of everyone else still in line. It would be wonderfully easy to gain recognition at these kinds of institutions, especially if not for merit. Maybe it was this accessibility to recognition that appealed to me.

This could very well be why John Patrick Shanley's *Prodigal Son* is one of my favorite plays.[9] It's a play about a young, troubled youth from the Bronx who finds himself on scholarship at a prep school, recognized for his exceptional talent in writing. The very system of the school, both the faculty and its students, begin to stir shortly after his enrollment. The lead character Jim Quinn, played by Timothée Chalamet in the off-Broadway premiere, is like the incarnation of an antibiotic. The headmaster of the school—played by Robert Sean Leonard who was actually the lead in *Dead Poets Society*—is, to complete the metaphor, the incarnation of bacteria. The two cannot coexist without conflict and ultimately—whether

---

8   Peter Weir, *Dead Poets Society*, (Burbank, CA: Touchstone Pictures, 1989. DVD).

9   Patrick Shanley, *Prodigal Son*, (New York: Theatre Communications Group, 2016).

in a minor or major way—the breaking down of the institution so that it may be restored to health.

Just as in *Dead Poets Society*—when an agent for change is introduced, when the sweetness of freedom is tasted—the greater whole cannot resist the impetus for change should the aforementioned agent be strong enough. The thought, conceived from a place I'm still very unfamiliar with, that I could be that agent for change was wildly exciting.

However, I didn't understand my attraction towards this until I got a bit older, and at this time, I felt I was only in it to earn the keys to the club. I made my decision, which seemed like the easier, more practical approach to all of it. I would go to Phillips Exeter or Andover or Choate, schools that boasted alumni of US presidents and world-renowned figures in all fields of work who now sent their kids and grandkids to these schools. And who was I? I was Jim Quinn. I felt I was a roughed up creative with a chip on my shoulder; I'd come in and take the school by storm. I'd be their star athlete and their scholarship student, or financial aid candidate at the very least, and I'd be the kid in the headmasters office every so often because I didn't adhere to the "lights out at 10 p.m." and "no beers on school grounds" rules or because I spoke derisively to a teacher. I was sold.

I interviewed with the representatives of these schools and emailed them in as proper a tone as I could summon up. I selected the top five prep schools in the country, according to the websites I had reviewed, and decided those were my options. I sent my highlight tapes and resumes to the coaches of the schools' basketball and football teams, academic records and passionately worded letters about why I would prove to be a positive fit in their institutions. My dad looked favorably upon this plan. He thought it would be great for a young man like myself and would instill tremendous character and work ethic. My mother, however, was skeptical about the whole thing, but I reassured her of this plan with persistence and confidence.

Soon, I began to tell my classmates about this plan when they asked. I told them I'd go to Andover or Exeter and then, after a year, go on to play Ivy League ball. They were impressed and confused. They didn't know about these prep schools because it was unheard of for someone to go to a prep school from my neighborhood. They asked if I really wanted to do another year of high school. I told them it was different—cooler, better, divergent from other options. By justifying the objective to my friends, I was also justifying the entire idea to myself. My intuition did its best to chime in countless times, but I didn't bother to listen.

When the time for admission responses came, I was at school just getting out of gym class. I checked my email, hands trembling.

"Dear Jet, we appreciate your application blah blah blah. However, we regret to inform you…"

My heart sunk into the soles of my feet. Two more emails were just like this one, and both of the others were rejections as well, one of them from Exeter. I felt sick to my stomach, angry, vulnerable, and now deeply insecure, but I was not going to cry in the gym locker room. My self-worth had plummeted in a way I had never felt before. There was only one thing to do in that moment—call my mom. I knew she'd know exactly what to say.

As expected, she told me there was no need to worry because things would work out exactly how they were supposed to. I hoped, with all I had, that she was right because I didn't apply to any safety schools. I didn't see myself as someone who needed an alternative plan because I thought I was good enough for anywhere and anything. I wasn't the kid who was picked last or excluded. Applying to these schools, I thought I'd be in free and easy and that the doors would be open for me with no hesitation.

In school a few days later, I received an email from the fourth school I applied to. I waited until the end of the day to open it, unable to focus on a single thing in class that afternoon. As soon as I got home, I ran upstairs into my room. I prayed for a few minutes before opening it, thinking that would do the trick.

"Dear Jet, blah blah blah. We regret to inform you…"

Again, I thought I wasn't as good of a person, student, or athlete as I previously thought I was. This was like playing one of those video games where your health is represented by a full bar on the corner of the screen. At this moment, mine had just about run out entirely. Now I felt I was not an exceptional enough human for their standards. I was not worth as much as their other students. I understood there was now only one option left standing on the table, and it wobbled before me. Maybe this meant my top choice, Andover, was the final option. I would hear from them and receive their acceptance with the utmost gratitude. I would accept this humbling experience and then pack my bags to head out East and start a brief life for myself at prep school. This was all just a lesson on the importance of being appreciative and of expunging my own hubris, right? That had to be it, and that's fantastic because now I understood! I was convinced and so was the rest of my family. Andover was the one.

Leaving a workout one morning, I felt my phone buzz as I walked through the high school parking lot towards my car. I knew. I knew it was them the same way you know when it's your parent calling. It's as though the phone buzzes differently. I pulled my phone out and saw the email notification. I walked quickly to my car, hopped into the driver's seat and shut the door. The dead silence was suffocating. I did not want to open the email. I felt the weight of what this email meant. It was my entire future in a single message and the consequences held me by the throat and began to squeeze. I felt I could cry, and I hadn't even looked at it yet. Pull it together, Jet! I summoned the courage to swipe my phone open, my hands shook fiercely.

"Dear Jet, blah blah blah. Unfortunately, we do not have space for a candidate like yourself at the moment..."

My body froze up. The breath left my body in one final exhale as it does when someone passes away.

Wait! Hold on!

"Unfortunately, we do not have space for a candidate like yourself at the moment, *but...*"

What's this "but"? I regained consciousness. There was some kind of reversal happening now. I found out I was waitlisted. Half of me took this as a hard no, that I should pack up my life and call it quits now, accepting a life of purposelessness and squalor. However, the other half saw this as a sign that I could show my commitment to the school and work my way through the thick mud of this waitlist into greener grass. I could do it. If anyone could do it, I could. Or at least, that's what my parents told me. I followed up with emails and updates as appealing as I could make them. I tried calling, but I was being ignored like I was some kind of clingy ex-boyfriend who won't let go of a relationship. I felt as though the admissions office saw my caller ID when I rang them up and said to each other: "It's him again."

They hid, seeming not want anything to do with the persistence I was devoting toward them, and they couldn't figure out how to let me down. So, I kept on until I got an email from the rep that said it wasn't looking good for me and I should plan for another school. She wished me the best.

I had been rejected by all five schools I applied to and was now nearing the very end of my senior year. Everyone else had committed to schools, and I had nowhere to even commit to. I had not taken any of the opportunities from the coaches who emailed me on behalf of smaller schools that were respectable but did not fit the vision I had created for myself. At this time, I wished I would've taken some of these coaches up on their offers, but it was too late. I could not come crawling back to them as a rebound.

I had to come to some kind of decision because the clock was winding down, but the problem was I didn't have any tangible options to decide from. I came up with the idea that I'd go to Santa Monica Community college for my first year and then transfer into USC. Maybe my mom was right—as she always was when it came to what was best for me—and I was not meant to go out east. Maybe I needed to follow my heart to California where my sister had found hers. I couldn't believe I was saying it, but I had no other options. I began looking into apartments and classes at Santa Monica, and the transfer program which matriculated into USC, but my dad was vigorously opposed to this plan.

I had picked USC because my sister went to school at Chapman, which was also in Southern California, and I knew kids who were already students at USC and had great things to say about it. I decided to take an official visit with my mother when I was a junior in high school during a trip to visit my sister; my mother and I walked around the campus in awe. It was the most beautiful place I had ever seen—a school out of a dream or a movie. With the sun, the campus, the flowers, the beautiful girls, and the respectability of it all, I felt it in my bones that I wanted to be at that school. It was like falling in love. There was both lust and adoration, an immediate congruence within the heart. I wanted everything to do with the school, and my mother desperately wanted me to apply. I told her I would, but I hadn't. I was convinced I needed to put all of my cards into the Ivy League basket and not accept anything less. She was not happy about this, but she said it was ultimately my decision. As much as I loved USC, I knew I wouldn't be able to play football there, and my ego was not letting go of that part of my identity.

Now I wished so bad that I had not been stubborn and just applied. It could've been my saving grace, but the reality was I had not applied and was left with no foreseeable plan for the next four years while everyone else was celebrating. At the very end of the school year, the last day of school, all of the seniors wear their college attire to represent the schools they'll be heading off to in the fall. I decided to wear a Santa Monica basketball shirt and USC shorts. My classmates were confused, as was I.

A few weeks later my dad came to me with "good news." I felt I had never needed "good news" more in my life.

"I got you a meeting at U of I."

"University of Illinois?" I asked facetiously.

This was my dad's alma mater.

"Yes. I called admissions and they said they make exceptions for certain late applications."

My ego caught a flame so wild and so hot it could've taken down an entire forest. Everything inside of me resisted, kicking and pushing the very idea away from where my ego stood tall, brazen, and arrogant.

It would be like going to my high school all over again, but with even more people I already knew. The mere idea of this made me want to punch and break things. I was a stubborn, ungrateful child, and my ego had blinded me to the reality of this. I, however, was not blind to the fact I really had no other option. My dad had to put me in my place.

"Jet, I don't know what you want me to tell you. You didn't get into the schools you applied to. This is a phenomenal school and, quite frankly, you don't have a choice."

Still, I fought back. My dad persisted.

"They have an unbelievable theatre program there. One of the best in the country."

"I've never heard about it! One of the best in the country and I've never even heard about it? How's that possible?"

"Jet…" my dad said in the cool, poised way he does when he wants to calm someone down. I certainly needed to be calmed down. He knew I was speaking and behaving from a place of deep insecurity. He knew I had been wounded by the way this had all unfolded.

"Jet. Their drama school has invited the both of us to go see their upcoming show. We're going."

I continued to argue until there was nothing left to argue. My father and I drove up to the campus a few weeks later for my audition into the theatre school. I still have a hard time believing I wore pastel pink shorts and a white polo shirt, embroidered with a big number three on the sleeve, that day.

I had prepared two monologues, one from Sam Shepherd, which I performed in a Bronx dialect for no good reason other than I thought it sounded cool, and another from *Othello*. I hadn't read either of the full plays. I had no idea how to properly prepare for an audition. In high school, I would just do what my acting teacher instructed and let "natural abilities" or sheer impulse do the rest of the work. I was not trained, and yet, I thought I was good because other people had told me so. That kind of validation, I have come to learn, is a dark and bottomless hole that leads to nowhere good.

We got to the school, its campus surrounded by miles and miles of cornfields, and I was ready to leave from the moment we parked. My dad, on the other hand, couldn't have been more excited to be back at his old stomping grounds. He walked me through different parts of campus, stumbling across golden nostalgia and occasionally stopped by thoughts that echo something along the lines of, "Where did the time go?"

I listened to all of his old stories from when he was at school there—the parties, campus jobs, girlfriends, and memories with friends he still speaks with today. My ego made it so hard for me to even hear the stories he was telling because it made me feel I needed to ignite some kind of conflict.

I liken the ego to the stubborn child at the park who refuses to enjoy the playground and the beautiful day because he couldn't have an extra snack that afternoon. He sacrifices the goodness before him for stale, self-made strife.

I stayed quiet. The heat was sweltering, and the humidity only exacerbated my pre-existing frustration.

"Jet, put your shirt back on for Christs sake, this isn't a gym. C'mon."

I acquiesced bitterly.

We walked up to the massive building that was the performing arts center. It must have been the biggest building on campus and caught me off guard. Inside, it was massive, brown, and vacant. It was a giant Starbucks of a building lobby, and there was not a soul there. It was summer, after all. My dad and I walked down the stairs into the lower level of the building where there were giant studios for all kinds of performance use. Along the walls were signed pictures of artists who had trained or performed there, expressing gratitude and love for the school and its faculty.

Soon we found the room I'd be auditioning in and we waited outside until one of the professors brought us in. My father and I introduced ourselves like we were a group, like he was part of the act and we would be performing together as a duo.

"Okay, I'll step out so you guys can talk," my dad said.

He had no idea how the world of theater really operated, and neither did I. There were three professors sitting at a table about twenty feet from me and the room was so big I began to feel it was swallowing me—these were my nerves kicking in. They asked me what I had prepared, and I informed them of my monologue choices.

"Great. Start whenever you're ready, and when you're done with the first, take a moment and go right into your second," said the skinny, somewhat British professor with a middle part and small glasses.

He seemed austere and unforgiving, and looking at him, I became even more nervous. I was instructed to start when I was ready, but now, I was unsure if I was even ready at all. I had to be good for people who seemed to expect nothing of me. These people who would rather be anywhere else, probably lunch, than in this room watching some unprepared young man in pink shorts and a sweaty white polo perform Sam Shepherd in a Bronx-ish dialect.

I stared directly into the eyes of one of the professors as I delivered the first monologue, having unexpectedly come to the decision that he would be my scene partner. I thought this would allow him to really feel the weight of my words as though I was speaking to him. It would be stronger because I had made this choice. "Choices," as we were told in our acting classes, were essential to acting. So, there was my choice, and in the moment, I was rather pleased with it.

After I finished "delivering" both monologues, they sat with blank and confounded expressions on their faces. They weren't quite sure what they had just seen. They saw Sam Shepherd in a Bronx-ish dialect and Shakespeare performed at an evidently low quality of understanding.

There was a brief silence before one of the other male professors—this one a little more gruff in appearance and bigger in stature, a man who looked like he had just finished hiking or, just as possible, was on his way to a hike—spoke up and started asking me some questions pertaining to the plays I had selected from. I summoned up responses as best I could, considering I hadn't read either of the plays. They knew I hadn't read the plays, so when they asked me, I did not lie to them about it. They gave me a handful of notes on the performance and some things to change for the next time I was going to do it for them. I agreed and gave it another go, and when I was done, they thanked me for coming in and I thanked them for having me. I walked out in my pink shorts, wet with a bit of butt sweat from sitting on a chair for my first monologue, and my fluorescent white polo. If this moment were a stage direction in a play it would read like this: *Exit EGO downstage right through door*—"Ego" being the character played by yours truly.

"How'd it go?" my dad asked casually, unsuspecting.

"It actually went pretty well, I think. They gave me some notes and I did it twice for them, but I think I did pretty well."

"Awesome. You hungry?"

"Starving."

We found a sandwich shop down the street and ate breakfast in this empty restaurant that had a nice vibe. It was quiet, dim, and smelled like idle coffee. My dad and I were the only two patrons in the place. He ate his potato chips at a high volume from across the table. I didn't seem to mind it as much as I thought I would. Having just performed, I was more at ease. There was catharsis from what I had done earlier, even if it was not great work. Having let go of something, although I wasn't quite sure what, created a pervasive sense of peace within me.

I wanted to leave after we ate, but we had that show to go to later on, so we wasted some more time walking around campus until it was time to head back over to the performing arts building. Now, the inside of the building was bustling with throngs of people who had come to see the show. The cafe in the lobby opened up and people were getting coffee and snacks. My father and I split a chocolate chip cookie before heading into the black box theater. As soon as we sat down, I liked what was happening on stage. The set was beautiful, made to look like the inside of a modern and refined upscale apartment on the Upper East Side of New York. For the next two hours, I was moved by the best piece of theatre I had ever seen. I had never cried during a play, but I cried at the end of this one. I couldn't believe how stellar these actors were, and the intimacy of the black box environment only heightened the experience. I badly wanted to be on that stage. I wanted to be a part of something as moving and real. I wasn't nearly on their level, but I knew I wanted to do everything I could to get there. I didn't tell my dad, though.

"What'd you think?"

He asked me now with some kind of expectation, because he knew what I thought—he had heard me sniffling throughout the show—and because this was all part of the persuasion.

"I thought it was incredible."

"So did I," he said. "Now let's get on home."

As we drove back, I envisioned myself on that stage at that school, walking the same campus my father walked forty years ago. I could see how excited he was at the thought of me going to school there, but I would have to accept the fact that I did not do what I said I was going to do— what I had told the kids at school, neighbors, and hospital staff I was going to do. I would be just another kid going to a school that everyone else was going to. I felt I was, in many ways, a disappointment to myself and considered the likeliness I would not even get into this school. Maybe I wouldn't go to college at all. I was unsure of all of this, but I knew I had fun performing earlier that day, and I wouldn't forget the play I had just seen.

Four weeks later I received an email notification from Illinois that read:

"Congratulations, Jet! You're an Illini!"

It felt great to be accepted, but I questioned who I was and what I was meant to be doing. I would have more time to search for these answers while in Champaign.

I accepted the school's offer and made my commitment to begin in the fall.

CHAPTER 9

OPEN CURTAINS

———

"Show us what you got, Jet!"

I was theatrical by nature, a kid with energy much bigger than myself and someone who was satiated by entertaining others. Maybe it was because I liked attention, or because I liked the immediacy and transparency with which you can tell whether or not you are impacting someone else. There is a great sense of meaning to be found within the ability to watch how my words and actions move someone else.

Because of my thespian-like idiosyncrasies, my mother was convinced of my destiny in theatre. I, although aware of the extent to which it brought me joy, refused to succumb to her pressure, too stubborn in my propensity for athletics. At this age, my friends habitually talked about things that were and were not cool, and theater was on the top of the not-cool list. Sports, on the other hand, ruled the former list, and I was very much dedicated to my pursuit of coolness. My mom, however, could not have cared less about my status seeking.

In one swift exemplification of this carelessness, she informed me the summer going into my freshman year of high school that I would be auditioning for a musical at my local theater. It was not up for discussion and was instead a matter I had no room to protest. I decided I would deliver the worst audition I could to jeopardize my chances of getting a part. For the audition, I was asked to prepare a song. However, I slyly asked my mom if I could rap instead. I assured her that there was singing in the chorus of the song I was proposing.

"I don't give a shit what you sing, Jet. Just as long as you sing," she told me sternly.

When we got to the audition, my mom asked the auditioner if it was okay that I chose a song with rapping; to my mother's delight, it was perfectly fine and conveniently enough there was actually a character in the musical who rapped. Typically, a parent does not stay in the room for an audition, but my mother was not one to abide by typical rules.

There were three of us: the auditioner, my mother, and me. The song I had chosen to prepare was "Practice" by Drake, which included lyrics like, "Girl you look good won't you back that ass up?"[10] There I was, in the clumsy throes of puberty, painfully reciting Drake lyrics for a middle-aged woman as proof of my talent, or lack thereof. The auditioner laughed and thanked me for coming by, and walking out, I silently counted my blessings for overcoming those awful thirty minutes of my life. I knew the suffering the three of us

---

10 Drake, *"Practice,"* (Track #17: *Take Care.* Young Money & Cash Money Records, 2011).

had just endured was well worth the reward of not having to step back into the theater. My mom would be disappointed, but she would have to learn to get over it. Two weeks later, the auditioner called my mother to tell her that I got the part. I was devastated by this news. My summer, as far as I knew it, was over, and to top it off I would have to explain to my friends why and how I ended up in a musical.

As soon as rehearsals began, I felt like a kid who had lost his parents in the mall. I was anxious and stewing in indignation. The rehearsals were long, time passing as slowly as it does at the DMV. For those of you who have seen *Interstellar*, I felt my situation was comparable to McConaughey's and Hathaway's circumstances when they first landed the planet referred to as Gargantuan and every hour was seven years on earth.[11] The building that housed the theater was damp and musty, which was partially justified because it was a community gymnasium by day and a music hall by night. If nothing else, the creative versatility of the space was inspiring.

In voice rehearsals, we trained to sing loud and ebulliently, my throat wearing out painfully after only a few minutes. I was by no means a gifted singer, so I did my best to stay quiet, my voice cracking underneath every couple of notes fortunately drowned out by the harmony of the rest of the ensembles' vibratos. Outside of rehearsal the cast enjoyed their downtime together, snacking, dancing, or chatting about the productions their schools were putting on in the fall. What was I doing during this free time? Distancing

---

11   Christopher Nolan, *Interstellar,* (Los Angeles, CA: Paramount Pictures, 2014, DVD).

myself and making sure that if a conversation did arise with another cast member, which it always did, I seized it as an opportunity to inform them that my mother had forced me into the production. Why would I tell the rest of the cast that? Because, at the time, I would rather have had them know my participation was no more than an act of pledgeship than for them to get the idea I was there of my own free will. Needless to say, I always have a good laugh about this now.

However, there was one detectable upside to becoming a part of the show—a silver lining— which happened to be our female lead Ana. She was resolutely captivating, the character you can't seem to take your eyes off of. During rehearsal, she'd be on stage dancing light on her feet and singing in a high, animated princess-like intonation. She was a Disney character that had come to life. I'd watch her from backstage, which was really just a kitchenette that doubled as an arts and crafts room, and my sense of time and place would slip away.

"Jet, this is your cue! Where you at, buddy?"

I'd run onto stage like I had hurried up from the downstairs area, feigning breathlessness—this was the best acting I did the entire production. I had to perform this whole "whoops, sorry I was downstairs!" bit on several occasions because, time and time again, I fell deep into the hypnosis of Ana's performance.

After a few weeks, and much to my surprise, I began to actually have fun at our rehearsals. I found commonalities with other cast members and learned to appreciate the catharsis that came with being a performer. I also found gratification in the realization that what I was doing was making my mom incredibly happy. Even though I found great joy in this, I was still stubborn and immature, meaning I was not going to give her the satisfaction of knowing how right she was for making me do this. I would have to work up to that moment slowly, gradually.

I waited all rehearsal, nerves building up in a crescendo, for when I had to come in and perform my rap, concluding with "Wall, out!" hitting a frozen pose like I was being photographed for an album cover. This never failed to garner applause from the crew, but every time they clapped, I smiled from ear to ear; I couldn't stay in character, laughing in delight at the applauses and at how ridiculous I thought I was. I found joy in the way people seemed to respect the absurd validity of my character and of me.

The intimacy of the theatre ultimately drew me in with the playfulness of it all, the empathy and the state of presence that was asked of us. The black box theatre was a small studio in which life was both created and recreated; the warmth of the stage lights overhead felt like the warmth of the spring sun, the crunch and creak of my feet meandering on the stage ground me in the awareness of the earth below, and the set props gave me the license to use my childlike imagination.

When I began high school, I took my first real acting class. My teacher often told us one saying:

"When you come into this theater, leave your ego at the door."

At the time, I only thought of the ego as something that inflated your sense of self-worth or contempt and I was committed to doing what he had asked of us. It wasn't until a few years later I realized just how important this was. By relinquishing the ego, an actor opens themselves up to the universal oneness inherent to the center of our very being. How could an actor sustain the ego during production and still fulfill, with exceptional quality of work, the role they are playing if the ego is working like a despotic director, telling us that we are different than all others? Acting, to an extent, is about closing the gap between the actor and the character so that the veil between the two is indistinguishable. How could an actor succeed in doing so when the ego relentlessly judges the very character they must empathize with? The ego—which says a person is worse or uglier or better than you—resists all forms of compassion. Our heart encourages us to try on the shoes of our neighbor, but the ego opposes it: "Don't put those shoes on. They stink and they don't fit you."

A question is asked of all actors in every role and every scene: "What do you want from this other person?" The answer is what is called "an objective" in acting jargon. The question "What can you give?" may sound inescapably selfish because it seems unconcerned with its generous opposite, but the objective could very well be "to comfort" or "to put at ease," which are not necessarily driven by selfishness.

If I declare my objective as "to win his approval," I must decide next how I will know I have accomplished this—what will the other character say or do to let me know I have achieved what I am after? The only way to know if I have succeeded is through checking in with how my tactics are working, to use my progression or regression in each moment of the scene to reach my goal. I must watch his eyes, hear the way his breathing may have changed, and listen to his words of protest or acquiescence to make this a real scene between two people; without my attention on this other character, there is no scene at all—it would simply be a monologue. The audience has presumably not paid to see self-indulgent rambling but rather to find entertainment in the natural cause and effect that creates the stories of our lives. Such is the necessity for altruistic storytelling.

The more time I spent in my efforts to do so, not-so-diligently practicing the art of compassion both in and outside of the studio, the more easily I began to connect to the surrounding world. I was able to find moments throughout my day when I felt I was really listening and observing others. I believe that because of this, I soon became the person my family and close friends could look to for guidance or comfort.

I felt I was able to lighten the burden of others simply by being present with them. I felt I was of service, which was ultimately all I wanted. I was convinced that, although this may have already been in my nature as it is for all of us, the theatre had provided the tools for me to become deeply human.

It wasn't until much later, listening to Pema Chödrön speak about the practice of tonglen meditation, that I realized why this was the truth. If we consider that an actor's job is to take on someone else's pain, suffering, desires, and passions, temporarily making them their own so they can share a heart with that person, and sometimes even bringing that person healing by doing so, then we can compare the work of the actor to the practice of tonglen. Chödrön describes it as such:

"We begin the practice by taking on the suffering of a person we know to be hurting and whom we wish to help. For instance, if you know of a child who is being hurt, you breathe in the wish to take away all the pain and fear of that child. Then, as you breathe out, you send the child happiness, joy, or whatever would relieve their pain. This is the core of the practice: breathing in another's pain so they can be well and have more space to relax and open, and breathing out, sending them relaxation or whatever you feel would bring them relief and happiness."[12]

In my first official high school production, I played the comic relief and was hooked.

Afterward, I auditioned for every production the school put on.

And now there I was, entering my first year of university not knowing how or why I had ended up where I was, but I was there nonetheless. In a strange way, I could feel that it was all as it should be. There was a bigger plan, one that cannot be jotted down on a daily agenda and crossed off at the end of the day, and I was only beginning to find out that such things existed.

---

12 Pema Chödrön, "Tonglen: Bad In, Good Out," (Lion's Roar, December 6, 2019).

CHAPTER 10

DRENCHED
IN UNCERTAINTY

———

It was pouring the morning I left for college, the kind of loud and dense rain that makes it difficult to see more than a few feet ahead.

For someone who seemed so confident to move on to "bigger things" and high school, I was nearly crippled by nerves when it came time to actually leave. I was so anxious my entire neck stiffened to the degree that I couldn't turn it without enduring nauseating pain.

Before I could even throw my bags in the car, my mother hugged me for what seemed like half an hour. When she finally let go, I assured her I'd be back soon and would only be two hours away.

"I know. You better come home to your momma!"

I did my best to act like I was ready to leave. However, the truth was that I felt like I wanted to stay home and live with my mom forever. The facade of toughness washed away, leaving behind not a single remnant of itself, and all that was left was the momma's boy who found comfort in being home in the very place he had sought to leave for so long.

I hugged and kissed my mother one more time for good measure before running out to the car.

"Oh wait! Don't leave yet! Jet, I forgot something."

She ran back up the stairs barefoot in her frequently-worn morning robe. After a few moments, she came running back down with a small box of golden sheen.

"Don't forget to use these."

It was a box of condoms.

She sent me off with a hug and a kiss on the cheek, and I nearly melted.

"Okay, sorry, I love you! Oh my god I love you so much it's sickening! Miss you already my sweet boy!"

She grabbed an umbrella by the door and opened it on our front steps, the umbrella blowing a bit in the wind as she tiptoed out to the car with me. Through the window, she addressed my dad in her usual sweet manner because—as she admitted to my sister and I from time to time—she still loved my dad immensely. As it was, he still loved her so deeply that it pained him to even see her.

"Bye, Steve. Drive safe. Love you," she said loudly through the cacophony of the rain pelting the car.

"Okay, Dena. We'll call you when we get all moved in," my dad replied.

Then we were off.

The closer we got to campus—the further from home—the more the rain lessened. I began to feel like I was suffocating. The uncertainty of my impending college life was like waking up in the middle of the night from shock—maybe from a nightmare or a noise or the exhausted recollection of something forgotten—only to see a moving shadow in your bedroom. Was that a knife this shadow was wielding? A gun? Something dangerous and fatal, but even this you could not be sure of. The only certainty is that your heart is nearly beating through your chest and you are preparing to either fight or accept death. Heavy exhalations during your final moments, until a few moments pass, and your vision focuses, bringing the realization that it had only been the shadow of a tree branch all along. All is restored back to rest.

Such is the power of our thoughts.

We arrived at my residence hall, lugging all that would comprise my room up the flight of stairs and placing it all at my door.

"Yo! You guys need a hand?" called out a kid two doors down, clearly already moved in from the look of his empty hands and the room key swinging from a Fighting Illini lanyard.

"I think we got it. Appreciate it, though," I replied.

"No problem man!" Now he was approaching, only a few feet away, hand out.

"Ibo. I'm your new neighbor," he followed up with palpable warmth and enthusiasm, as though we had already been friends for years. I already liked this kid and the way his familiar energy put me at ease.

It was no mystery then how Ibrahim, who went by Ibo, soon became my closest friend at school. He and I essentially did everything together that first year. I needed to play and run around like a puppy for my well-being. Sometimes, I would go from playing tennis to basketball to soccer in the same day, and it was all cathartic and meditative for me. Ibo was up for all of it. He didn't care so much for his schoolwork, sleeping and missing classes if he felt like it, never seeming to accumulate any stress. I found out not long into the year that I was not one to stress over school either. I made sure I got my work done and I had good grades, but I prioritized my well-being above all.

I quickly developed the belief that my life, as is all of ours, was incalculably bigger than a GPA or exam score, and Ibo seemed to recognize this in his own way. He was a smart kid, in school on a scholarship, but his identity did not revolve around his role as a student.

It took about a week to get into my groove at school and when I did, my neck loosened up completely.

I went through the whole fraternity process until, half-way through pledging late into the semester, I decided it was not for me. I felt real affection and respect for the kids I had met in the fraternity, my "brothers," but at the end of the day, the exclusivity of it all was not appealing. However, I had the good fortune of meeting some incredible friends during the time I pledged, friends who surprised me with their love and support when they found out my mother was not well at home and encouraged my pursuit of acting.

The fraternity even let me perform for the whole house. One night at chapter dinner, me and a few of my friends performed the dinner scene from *Scarface*. The four of us had rehearsed the entire week, everyone putting their best effort in, and when the night came, Jake, playing the role of Elvira, threw water in my face as the scene reached its climax. Almost everyone in the room had already seen the movie, but there were audible gasps at that moment followed by riotous applause and shouting.

It was a beautiful reminder there is a universal and inescapable appreciation for life and art of all forms. This was, without a doubt, one of the fondest moments of my life.

However, in my actual theatre classes, I was not as big of a hit. Before dropping from the fraternity, I was going out and drinking frequently, which was not conducive for my 8 a.m. acting classes. I was also doing the bare minimum when it came to the work we were assigned, frequently making an unintentional fool of myself in class. As much as I didn't feel right about my new academic habits, I was enamored with my social life.

Things continued on like this for almost the entire first semester, but, after all, wasn't this what college was about?

CHAPTER 11

THE WAY HOME

After a few months of school, I found myself longing to get back home and return to all of the things distance had reminded me I love.

Fortunately, it was that time of year when school lets out for winter break, and I had my train ticket back to Chicago booked a week in advance.

I lugged my duffle bag, so heavy it wouldn't stand a chance against airline regulations, through the Urbana train station. People stared like I was dragging a corpse around; they were appalled and bewildered. Some—like myself—were impressed with my packing capabilities. I had taken the train before, but today was an unusually busy day. It was December 8 and I couldn't help but wonder if it was a national holiday for Amtrak travel, or maybe I missed out on some sort of winter clearance sale for train tickets.

I was not fond of the throngs of people waiting, the dense heat they created, and the fact that they couldn't just drive to where they were going. The reality was I was just as much, if not more, a contributor to this problem. My state of irritation only grew worse upon my effort to accept I wasn't going to be able to sit by myself on the train like I planned. If I knew then what I knew now, I would know that this was my ego chiming in to judge and complain about the situation.

Earlier, I was certain I'd have a pair of seats to myself because I believed I had become a master in the art of making a seat look unavailable. In this art, there are two primary methods, one being the "Put both headphones in and do angry eyes while staring out the window." This approach shows people you're not in a good place emotionally, and they may even become the target of your apparent unpleasantness. The second method is the "Put as much shit as possible in the seat next to you," which must then not be moved until everyone has found their respective seats.

That day, neither of those options were accessible. As soon as I got on the train, I could see all seats had already been occupied by at least one person. I accepted my fate and made my way down the aisles, looking for a seat mate, possibly even a friend. I glided down the narrow aisle past a girl with a face much younger than her college apparel suggested and an older gentleman mumbling to himself. I enjoyed my more active version of people-watching until I found myself drawn to a man in grey sweatpants and a white long-sleeve t-shirt. He was a smaller fellow of about thirty years, the light from the window illuminating the three teardrop tattoos directly below his left eye.

He looked up as I made my way closer. He had a beseeching look on his face so prominent I disregarded the fear of violence I had been programmed from a young age to detect from his tattoos. While dropping into the seat next to him, I accidentally bumped into his shoulder, prompting my sense of obligation to deliver an apology. For some reason, I wasn't able to verbalize one. He knew I was sorry.

I inspected the teardrops and the ink that embroidered his hands, forearms, and neck with depictions of Christ and other names written in cursive. Naturally, I had questions. I would, should I find the opportunity, ask him what the teardrops signified—if they denoted what I believed they did—and when the last time he cried was. I felt a compulsion to ask him when the last time his real tears rolled over their permanent shadows, and if his hands—covered in sanctified words and images—had betrayed themselves through nefariousness. He reached down into a big plastic bag—the only bag he had with him—not long into the ride and grabbed two wrapped candies. He turned toward me with the innocence of a young child and a clear intention to speak. I took out a headphone to receive his question:

"You want one?" he asked with that same innocence.

He was soft spoken, on the verge of sounding nervous as though he were the new kid in school just trying to make a friend.

This piece of candy could best be described as "unidentified." It was a red hard candy wrapped in thick, unlabeled plastic that looked more like wax than anything. I was not a candy person, and I felt my compass, ingrained with the advice to never accept candy from strangers, jolt into service. I politely declined the offering but thanked him anyway. There he and I sat, previously not knowing anything about each other besides him knowing I don't like candy, and me knowing that he's generous.

We sat there together while he nodded his head softly in rhythm with the music on his MP3 player, rarely taking his eyes off of the tirelessly transitioning scene outside of the train window. I became increasingly more eager to know about him. I just watched him out of the corner of my eye for a bit as he stared out of the window, restrained amazement reflected in his eyes. He was holding something in, but I could tell he too was anxious to get back to something. He turned to me again after some more time had gone by to ask if I would send a message for him using my phone, which I gladly agreed to do.

"Beto will be at Union Station at 1:30 p.m." *Sent.*

He justified his request by informing me he didn't have a phone. I took his willingness for conversation as a window to follow my curiosity forward one inch at a time. I had a long list of questions for him, but I wanted to play it cool. I asked him harmlessly if he was from Chicago, to which he responded yes.

"So, what were you doing back in Champaign?"

He replied with chagrin:

"I just got out of prison today."

My surprise prompted him to continue, "Five-and-a-half years."

"Wow," I replied, at a loss for words.

He and I continued our conversation, him beginning to divulge more about his experience in prison.

He said he worked in the kitchen during his time and developed a lot of baking skills. He also explained that the candy he offered earlier was made at the jail and could be bought for a quarter. Most things could be bought, he explained. I asked if he had family, and he told me about his stepchildren who were waiting with his wife at the train station. He told me he was very excited and unexpectedly nervous to be back home. I told him I was, too. I then felt incredibly silly for saying that. He told me he was going to find himself a job and never get put in prison again. I asked about the food and he described the unpalatable menu. I nearly joked that the food at my school was probably no better, but thankfully, I refrained. I asked about the guards and he told me some were loud and harsh. I never asked him how he ended up there, even though I could see his anticipation of the question. I never asked about the teardrops, either. That conversation would have to be for another day—maybe in another life—should we cross paths again.

Before we pulled up to the station, he offered me that same piece of candy. I felt obliged to accept this time, so I did. After all, he didn't seem as much a stranger anymore. The candy tasted the same as a watermelon jolly rancher, only it was bigger and stuck to your molars more.

"Now you can tell your friends you ate candy from a jailhouse."

He laughed and looked back out the window with a polite, unassuming smile.

The train pulled into Union Station and we got up together, shook hands, and wished each other a happy holiday.

He and I had once sat there not knowing anything about each other, but we got off the train knowing both of us we were glad to be home.

PART TWO

THE EGO, AND I

CHAPTER 12

SON, WE'RE GOING TO NEED YOU TO JUMP

All kinds of treatments for my mother were being tried, but there was a great deal of backfire.

There was more fighting and kicking and running around desperately, but she didn't look like herself. By my freshman year of college, our walks became slower and she breathed much heavier because she was tired, worn out from the efforts to save her own life.

Through her research, she found a doctor in Germany who performed the kind of immunotherapy treatment she was looking for. She booked a one-way flight.

Three weeks later, I was waiting to pick her up outside of O'Hare International Airport, keeping a close watch on the terminal door. I saw a woman being pushed out in a wheelchair, sitting deflated, head down and neck bent significantly to the right. My heart hurt intensely when I saw people like this. The chair was now being pushed further from the airport and closer to my car, and I soon realized that it was my mother being pushed in the chair.

My heart plummeted, shattering and strewn across the dirty, frozen pavement. I searched for a breath to take but with no success until my tears brought it out from me, my mother now crying hysterically as she approached. I could see that the young man pushing her toward me wanted to cry too. I remember thinking I would've understood if he had.

When the tears stopped, my mother assured me she was not giving up yet.

She began even more therapy. Everyday, she'd have lymphatic drainage, physical therapy, or treatments at the hospital. Anything she could do to take her life back—she was doing it. She frequently began to ask my sister and I if she was going to make it this time, telling us how she didn't want to go yet and how she badly wanted to see what her grandchildren would look like; each time, Paris and I reassured her she would.

She could still walk, but her legs became so feeble that she was very limited in mobility. I told her she'd have her strength back again—praying every day to myself that this was true—and that for now, it was okay I had to carry her up the stairs to her room. I would carry her a hundred miles if I had to.

My mother now had purple and green tumors that covered her entire chest and her upper back, which I could barely stomach the sight of, and her left arm was swollen so intensely she started calling herself Popeye. However, I had a difficult time finding the humor because of how deeply disturbed I was.

For the first time in my mom's life, she needed to be cared for around the clock, and I could see how much she resented it. My mother was the caretaker, not the person who needed to be cared for. She was the eternally active, badass mom who ran, worked out with her kids, and played basketball on the trampoline with her son, not a frail, bedridden woman. She told my sister that when she got better, when she returned to the way she was, we would have a big celebration as a family.

I was now home for Christmas break during my first year of college, and I spent the first week of break hanging around the house with my mom, watching television, making sure she was taken care of, and trying to communicate what my mother needed to the new caretaker Paris had hired.

"Tacos. Yeah, she likes these tacos from a place a few streets over—actually, never mind I'll just go grab 'em. I'll be right back," I didn't trust this woman with the demands of my mother because, as a matter of fact, I didn't think anyone could successfully handle the demands of my mother.

My mother demanded perfection, and nothing less.

She had an affinity for the tacos at a local restaurant called Mean Weiner, a small hidden Mexican joint with great food. My mom never ate this kind of food, and if she did, it would only be a bite or two. Yet she loved Mean Weiner, and my sister and I loved that she loved it. It became our spot.

Slumped on the couch, I laid the food out for my mother to eat. I watched her eat, each bite laborious. I had learned to put a small towel under her chin because she often spilled food on herself now that only the left half of her mouth still had function.

Watching her, I couldn't even believe I knew this woman. She looked familiar, like a face at an extended family gathering your intuition tells you has been around since you were too young to remember, but still you struggle to recall a name or where, exactly, you've seen them.

This woman sits on the couch exactly where my mother would sit, only this is not my mother. She lays there stiff, her silhouette minimized by the light coming through the sliding doors behind her, releasing brief and audible exhalations of pain ever so often. She looks terribly uncomfortable. This woman cuddles with ice packs and worn-down reading glasses, although she hasn't read anything since I started watching her.

I've known this home and all passersby since we bought the place, but I have never seen this face.

There was only one woman who ever regularly walked these rooms and sat in these chairs, but I dare not say who, for I fear even by remote comparison, I would be stripping that woman of her dignity. The woman I'm thinking of didn't just walk these halls, she danced through them. She brought this house to life and made it a home. I swear, if you could see the way she owned every step with unbroken confidence, tiptoeing up the stairs in a way worthy of ballet slippers and the accompaniment of a classical piano. If you could see it, you would know what I mean. Even when she said nothing, she was heard. Her energy unwavering and posture so straight that when she moved, it appeared as though she was cutting through the air with the grace and precision of a fine blade.

She could cook. She was as strong and bold as they come. She spoke with presidents and wrestled with bears. She saved the lives of people who had already assumed their fate with despair. She looked death in the face and said 'Fuck. Off.'

Now, woman of mystery existed in her place, beaten and broken down by a force much greater than man, a force with an ugly face and a bruting attitude like that of a scornful general. She struggles to speak and when her eyes move, they do so with great and slow distinction because nothing else on her face moves.

She looked over at me and asked for a glass of water—I obliged. As I got closer, I could see the purple tumors that covered her chest and neck. I tried not to stare because of how devastating it looked, but she grabbed my hand once I had gotten closer, holding onto me, and told me how much she loved me. As tears began to leak down her cheek, I was never more certain of who she was. This was a moment I prayed would never come.

"Please don't forget about me."

My words barely found enough strength to carry themselves. "I won't, mom."

Later, once she had closed her eyes for a nap, I went up to my room and closed the door, sat on my bed in silence with my head in my hands, tried to process where life had taken us, and grappled with the violence with which my mother's illness now tortured her. I asked The Universe quietly to give my mother the strength to push through and get healthy again, and for the equanimity to surrender to the fate It had already created for us. I often found conflict in not knowing which to pray for. I was either pleading gently for health and recovery or asking for the serenity to put my trust in life, regardless of the outcome. But because this was my mother, I did not want to give her up. I did not want to lose the woman who gave me life.

The sun was out the next day, but it was cold. My mother, however, felt she needed to get outside for a walk. I dressed her warmly and we walked out into the harsh chill of mid-December.

We made our way down the street very slowly, my mother putting nearly all her weight against me. I didn't want to think of how weak her legs felt at the time, for I feared if I did, the strength from mine might forsake me too.

"Fuck, it's freezing," she said from under her scarf.

I responded through a freezing, stiff mouth, "I know."

"Once I beat this fuckin' thing we're going somewhere warm."

For the first time in my life, something not so deep within me wasn't sure about another victory.

"Absolutely, mom. We will."

I was unsure of myself, the hope in both my voice and heart running on an empty tank.

We only got to the end of our street before having to turn back; she was too tired and cold.

Her arms were wrapped tightly around mine, as though she was holding on for her life. She was.

That was the last time I walked down Lorenzi Lane with my mother.

I left for California the next morning because I had a ticket to visit Paris for a few days.

We had planned to spend Christmas with the family of one my mother's closest friends since high school who now lived in San Diego. My mother and I had stayed with her several times before, so I had grown relatively comfortable around her and her family. She was the kind of woman who always left her front door unlocked, her faith in the goodness of people overcame any fear of nefariousness. She possessed a kind of robust and unbiased warmth that put you at ease.

Paris was now a junior in college and lived in a disaster of a two-story house with a few of her friends. She had also just recently gotten herself a husky puppy whom she named Atlas, and I was eager to meet him.

I had obvious concerns, however, about leaving my mother at home with the caretaker.

"Don't worry about me, Jet. I'll be here. You go have fun with your sister!"

The last time I had been to California was to visit schools with my mom. She and I visited USC where we were walked around the gorgeous landscape with a group of other visitors while my eyes covetously observed the students who were enrolled and making their way to class.

"Damn. I feel like I want to go to class right now," I said to my mom.

"So, let's go."

"No, I mean, I'm just saying I love it here. We can't actually go into a class right now."

"Why not?"

"Because we're not students, ma. Why else do you think?"

"Oh, stop it. Let's go find a class."

She parted from the group and I had no choice but to follow. We were off on our own way, neither of us knowing where we were going, but my mom walked as if she had been to the campus a number of times before. She walked into the School of Cinematic Arts, and I was starting to get a bit nervous, but I didn't bother to protest because I knew better.

She found a lecture hall and cracked the door open to peek in. I prayed that she wouldn't walk in, but, of course, she did. Like a heat seeking missile, she located two seats in the back immediately and staked our territory without hesitation. I followed clumsily, feeling like a kid who skips school only because the "cool kids" are doing it and he doesn't want to be left behind.

My mother and I sat down while a few students in the row side-eyed us, but she paid them no mind. I sunk far into the chair while trying to look confident. I was playing the role of student who brought his mother to class because she's in town visiting—student without a backpack or any notebooks that is. I tried to sell it with the eyes, but I don't think there was a single one of the onlookers who bought it.

My mom and I sat there for about twenty minutes listening to a middle-aged man in a rather oversized button-down lecture about the fundamentals of producing a feature film. My mom listened, enthralled, and then leaned over to me and said:

"This is where you have to go to school, Jet."

After a minute of processing what she had said, I smiled and leaned toward her.

"I agree."

After we left the class it was just her and I, free from any predetermined agenda, and it was beautiful outside, as it always is in Southern California. We had found ourselves in one of the courtyards of the Cinema School that boasted benches soaked in sunlight and a large, square grass yard.

"Let's sit for a second," my mother suggested.

We both sat on one of the benches and she looked up at the sun and closed her eyes. I watched her, smiled, and did the same. I could hear the sounds of the campus now. The birds singing, wheels of longboards carving up pavement, the flowing water from the fountains behind us, and the breeze rustling through the palm trees.

It felt good to be back in California after many months away, but there was a heaviness in me this time. I felt uneasy about being away from home and worried about how my mom was holding up alone with the caretaker.

It was Christmas Day and we were at Sarah's ex-husband's house, where their family made breakfast and sweets and wore matching pajamas. My sister and I did our best to act comfortable, but we were not. The family gathered around to open expensive presents and were generous enough to have given a present to both Paris and me. These were thoughtful and decent people, but the warmth of their family was not enough to conquer the concern that had overcome both Paris and me.

After the unwrapping of gifts, we all walked out to the garage at the far end of the long brick driveway to see the father's cars and take pictures of all the kids. Paris and I watched with feigned amusement before her phone lit up with a call from our mom.

Paris stepped away from the rest of the family, and I followed. Her face stiffened, and I felt my stomach drop.

Paris looked at me, tears welling and until her eyes looked like glass.

"Mom just called freaking out. She said she couldn't swallow, and she called dad to help her and now he's taking her to the hospital, but she doesn't want to go to the hospital because— because she said they were going to try to kill her."

In that moment I had seen, superimposed, both the six- and twenty-two-year-old Paris wipe her tears with her palm. In that moment, I was both the boy I had been and the young man I was becoming.

We left the Christmas gathering shortly thereafter and headed back to Paris' house in silence, although I could feel she and I were thinking the same thing: how much time, exactly, did our mother have left?

My dad called and assured us he was taking care of everything at home as he always does. My father is the incarnation of Atlas, the Greek god who carried the world on his shoulders. He is the embodiment of endurance and resilience. When someone needs something done, they can count on Steve to take care of it without any expectation for reimbursement. My father lends a hand to others, even if it may jeopardize his own well-being, which is why this quality can, ironically, become one of his greatest downfalls. At times, I wondered if Paris named her dog Atlas to always feel, to some capacity, like she was near our father.

The reality now, however, was that this was not a situation my dad could simply take care of.

Later that night, he told Paris and I we needed to catch a flight back home the next day.

Paris and I packed up and headed to the airport early the next morning. The flight was seemingly endless. For hours, I sat with my eyes closed, praying my mother would be fine, but my intuition was already in mourning.

My dad picked us up from the airport, maintaining composure the best he could for the three of us. The anxiety in the car was palpable and oppressive.

We pulled up to the hospital, but before we got out of the car my dad stopped and looked at Paris and me.

"I just want to let you both know before we go in that she can still hear and feel you, but she's unresponsive now."

I only partially knew what that meant; I thought my father meant she was only currently unresponsive, but she would come out of it after a short while like a nap, but soon I realized she was in hospice care. I remembered that my grandpa Nate, my dad's father, had been placed in hospice care when I was in eighth grade before he passed away. I remember Googling the word "hospice" before visiting him at the hospital and reading that it was really a place where terminally ill people went to pass away without feeling any pain.

The garish white hospital was a shock to the senses as it always is. My hands were trembling and sweating, and my heart beating was so hard into my chest I thought it was creating a cavity.

We walked through the long halls, nurses smiling at us along the way.

Stop fucking smiling, I thought to myself.

We arrived at the room. The glass door was closed and there was a curtain covering it. My sister stepped in with Atlas—who she had brought along—and seconds later, I heard her break down into hysterics. My father waited outside with me. I didn't want to go in. I couldn't move. It was like being at the edge of a cliff, knowing you had to jump but having no idea what was beneath you. I presumed it could only be sharp rocks. If I stepped into that room, it would be over. Whatever was waiting in there would become my reality, and it was an inescapable one. I had no choice.

I walked in, my dad following a step behind. As soon as I saw her lying there, a frail and pallor remnant of the mother I knew, the tumors all over her chest dark and black now and the life gone from her face and skin, my bones turned to dust.

I felt my legs give out beneath me, and my heart sunk to the unchartered basement of the hospital.

I imagined this was what it felt like to be hit by a small SUV.

A nurse with zero social conscientiousness stepped in and asked if we needed another chair moments before her cell phone started ringing. I wanted to throw her cell phone through the window. I shot her a look that said, *"Get the fuck out of here,"* and it seemed my message was clear, because she embarrassedly left. Ten minutes later, she returned back to see if we needed anything.

Yeah why don't you get us some fucking crackers and an apple juice, I thought. I knew my mother would have laughed at that. She was always adamant about keeping her passing as lighthearted as possible, so maybe this moronic nurse was actually just my mother's way of facilitating that request. Either way, I was not entertained.

After about twenty minutes of being beside my mother and sister, holding onto her delicate hands, now soft and light as a feather from their lack of vitality, I had to step out. My dad followed, and we had a long embrace out in the hall where I cried into my father's arms the way I had wanted to for a long time, although certainly not under these circumstances. When we finally separated, a nurse had passed us and smiled.

"What the fuck are these nurses smiling at. I don't fucking get it. It's ridiculous," I said to my dad.

"They're just trying to be comforting," he replied, almost like an apology on their behalf.

"You don't have to stay here. I understand if you can't," he told me.

"I just can't look at her like this. I know she wouldn't want me to remember her this way. I know it."

"Okay, let's step outside."

We did.

The doctor had told us that my mother would not make it through the night, but, as per usual, my mother made it through the next five days, unresponsive but somehow summoning the strength to keep kicking the sheets off of herself as though she was trying to make an escape.

I returned back to the hospital only once but could not see her without feeling my heart was being ripped from inside of me. I decided I could not see my mother like that anymore. Paris, however, stayed with her nearly all day and night for each of those five days, grooming her, reading to her, and watching episodes of *Sex and The City* with her as they often did together.

"Jet, get your ass in here and watch *Sex and The City* with your sister and I," my mom would say, calling out from her room where we'd all watch movies together in her bed.

I didn't get much from the show other than that the women could suck down Cosmopolitans like fish do water.

It wasn't until the late hours of January 2nd that my mother had officially graduated from this life.

That night, I laid in Paris' bed crying until I fell asleep. Paris did not cry again for another six months.

I wrote this in the notes of my phone the night before my mother passed away:

"I just want you to understand this more than anything. I want you all to feel this for us, with us. I don't wish for you all to endure it the same way, that is one wish I will never make, but if you could feel this beside me, all of us holding one another, that would be enough. And excuse me because my thoughts run wilder than drunk fraternity boys while I attempt to write them down with any sort of structure that can be understood, but if I can be clear about one thing, it is that this is NOT just about me. In fact, it is the opposite.

It's maddening to want to express this but to constantly feel as though the words I write and speak to you mean nothing. How could I let that happen? How could I allow these words to fall without weight? I promise I'll do my best to prevent that. The moments before me now are surreal and yet not real even in the slightest sense. I am left here to discover myself now drifting in an ocean of contradiction where the waves push themselves away from shore rather than towards it. Something is not right, but I can see peace further out where the sun kisses the water.

Please just hold my hand now, and feel the heat behind my uneasy breath. Hold my hand now and let these tears dry when they will. Hold my hand now and let us give praise for the life before us because it was a full one. Because it was a life that was not spent in fear and because it was not artificial.

Because it was beautiful and organic and honest. And there was love. You must know how much love we shared with one another. You must know how strong that is. How can I capture something as powerful as that for you? I don't know if I will ever find the answer to that question, but I do know that I will make the effort to search for it. And you'll have to learn to forgive me in the case that I never find such a thing, or, at the least, you may come to the understanding that this moment is not something that can simply be grabbed and given away. It is not something that is meant to be pawned off or stretched for the sake of a compelling story but rather something that needs to be cradled with just enough delicacy.

I'd like to believe there is a way to encompass the limitlessness of this all, as much as it might not seem possible, or logical for that matter, but for now I can only wish that you might extend a hand or nod your heads or offer eyes that avow something like: *'I know what this is like for you.*

I can see it in your face. I can feel that in your chest. That unspeakable density that rests within you.'

If I saw that in you, I know I'd be able to breathe easier. But there's something prodding at the bottom of my stomach that tells me you should already know all of this. That you had known I was going to write this, and you won't think that I'm asking much of you because, for a long time, you've anticipated these requests. Because you already knew how right all of this is.

But if you didn't, I don't resent you for it.

All I ask is that you stand with me now and feel this heart of mine that aches with gratitude."

CHAPTER 13

THE CEILING IS LEAKING

———

The night after my mom passed away, my dad brought dinner over to the house for me, Paris, my grandmother, and two of my mother's dear friends, Sarah and Beth, who had flown into town a few days before. Sarah joined my mother a few months later after unexpectedly dying. Eating didn't feel like the right thing to do, nor did anything else really, but I ate a small portion because it was in front of me and I didn't want to make any sort of trouble by not eating.

Even though I didn't eat much, my stomach turned violently and felt overfilled, as though I had pushed it to its very limit. I excused myself from the table and got into bed early, hoping I'd be able to sleep. For hours I laid awake, trying to find the perfect position, holding onto my stomach to try and ease the intense pain.

That pain eventually transmuted into nausea; I rushed as quietly as I could to the toilet so as to not wake everyone that was already sleeping, shut the door, and began throwing up. It was the kind of vomiting that comes with a serrated burning deep in the chest and stomach, but I can remember thinking vomiting was more appropriate at the time than eating. So I threw up the entire night with the faint hope that maybe if I threw up enough, my mom, who was always there for me when I threw up—to lay with me in bed afterward and ease me into sleep with one of her gentle back massages—would come back to console me. She did not. I sat there alone, crying quietly, wishing that this was not how it had to happen, wishing life could have unfolded differently so I would not have wound up lying in front of the toilet without a mother.

This was my victim response kicking in, asking life questions like "why me?" and "why couldn't it have been different?" and all kinds of other persistent complaints about "unfairness." The reality was that this was just the way it was supposed to be, the very agenda my mother and I had thanked The Universe for. How could I feel indignation for something I had been expressing appreciation to for years? This was the plan. This was the gift, even if it was not readily understood by its recipients.

After a short while, Paris opened the bathroom door to all my half -naked sorrow. Her deep concerns were met with an explanation of food poisoning; she ran quietly downstairs to our medicine cabinet, retrieving the remedy my mother used to soothe our stomachs, and when I finally made it back to my bed, she laid beside me until I fell asleep.

The next day, I woke up exhausted and deeply grieving, still without an appetite and now enveloped by an empty house. Everyone had already begun their day tending to everything that needed to be taken care of. I could never have imagined just how much work needed to be done when someone passes away—it's enough work qualify as its own occupation, albeit an undesirable one.

Not long after I made my way downstairs, my grandma walked through the door. Seeing her, I felt like someone who had just been stranded on an island seeing another person for the first time in months. I had just seen my grandmother last night, but when I woke up that morning to stark silence, I felt like I had lost my entire family. I felt I was drowning, and my grandma became my life raft. I sat down on the couch while she made me some toast, telling me I needed to eat something. I ate a few bites to appease her, but I could tell she was not satisfied by any measure. She joined me on the couch, and we tried, rather desperately, to find a movie to watch.

Nothing sounded appealing. I needed noise, distraction, an escape, anything besides what I was feeling, but I had reached a narrow dead end and it became disturbingly clear there were no viable options for getting out. There was no choice other than to accept and sit with this feeling for a while, although it was dark and heavy and deeply painful.

We'd select a movie and I'd have to change it after ten minutes because I didn't think it was the "right" one. She reached over and grabbed my hand, holding it in hers. She knew I was in need of comfort and relief from this asphyxiating pressure. I decided that a shower would do me good.

Immediately upon stepping into the warm stream of my shower, I began to sob. I was pained by the thought of life without my mother. I was pained thinking about how she had to live without her brother, pained by the understanding that I was not the only one who was enduring this kind of suffering. There were millions of people in the world who felt the pain I was feeling now. I cried in anticipation of seeing a close friend of mine, and what his hug would feel like; I felt I needed that hug more than anything. After what must have been thirty minutes, I turned the shower handle, the stream came to a stop, and I stepped out to dry myself off. While doing so, I noticed the floor was wet, so I threw my towel over it before getting dressed and heading back downstairs.

In the living room, my grandma had also put a towel on the floor with a bucket on top of it.

"Jet, the ceiling started leaking."

The water from both my tears and the shower had flooded the bathroom, made its way into the floor's air vent, and seeped through the living room ceiling.

When I returned to school after winter break, I decided that I was going to do something for my mom each day.

I would concentrate any ambition I had into doing right by her. I had one primary goal at this time, and that was to make her proud. I knew if I wanted to do so, I would have to, as she would say, "kick my shit into gear."

I took on a conviction—one that I was almost entirely unfamiliar with—when it came to my studies and thankfully I did, because next semester I had an acting teacher who left no room for the excuses I made first semester. It was the best gift I could've asked for. As much as I always had trouble with authority, it was obvious to me that, ironically, I was someone who blossomed from discipline.

After my first performance in class, my teacher began to ask questions about the scene and my character, but I had not come prepared with answers.

"Jet, if you think you're just going to get through my class with your *joie de vivre,* then you're in for a rough wake up call."

He didn't need to say more than that. I never came unprepared again. I got to class early every morning to warm up, rehearsed at night when my classes were over, and worked through acting-specific exercises at home. My mother desperately wanted to see me perform on stage and become the young man she felt I was destined to be, and that is exactly what I devoted myself to doing.

I also began practicing yoga and meditation more frequently than I ever had. I found myself in a qigong class once again, but this time, it was not the same. This time I had come into it open-minded and ready for whatever work we were going to be doing. It was life changing. I started to actually learn and feel my way through this art and found it allowed me to tap further into my source of energy and joy, to develop a better understanding of what I and others were going through, furthering my feeling of compassion toward myself and others. This practice allowed me to find moments of surrender. Through qigong, I found my mind, heart, and body could move more freely than ever before, and it brought the world into greater clarity.

This practice encouraged the feeling that life was working with me, that we were close friends who wanted the best for one another.

In this clarity, I could see that as incredible as this year at school was, I wouldn't stay in Illinois when the year was over. I had been holding close to my heart the liveliness I felt in Southern California and the beautiful memories of the lecture hall where my mother and I came to the understanding that USC was the school for me. I had several dreams of her and I walking around campus, of me leaving class and meeting her somewhere beneath the palm trees in the warm light of the sun.

I submitted my transfer application along with prayers it would be received positively, and in the middle of one week during that semester, I packed a bag to go back to Chicago where I was scheduled to audition for the school of drama at USC.

As I was leaving my dorm room, Ibo had come see what I was up to.

"Where you going bro?"

"I got the audition for USC, remember?"

"Oh, shit that's right. So, you're about to get on a train back home?"

"Yeah bro… you wanna come?"

"You serious?"

"I was joking, but if you actually wanna come then pack a bag and let's do it bro! Train leaves in an hour."

He thought to himself for a second and decided, "Uhhh, yeah, fuck it, I don't really have any work to do. Lemme just pack some clothes."

He threw some clothes into his backpack and we were on our way.

It was my first time being back home after my mom had passed, and I was overcome by a tidal wave of grief.

My dad came by that night and did his best to do something thoughtful, as he always does, even if the thought may not be in any way comprehensible. His thoughtful gestures don't always come across the way he expects. As an example, he might pick me or Paris up from the airport and bring a slice of cheesecake, even though neither of us particularly like cheesecake. The thought is undoubtedly there, but it is often wildly random.

This habit also manifests itself in his cooking, culminating a meal that consists of food groups never paired together before. That night, my dad made one of those meals, and I found myself growing frustrated watching him cook, my anxiety intensifying rapidly and heart thudding quick and heavy.

I excused myself from the kitchen, got into my car, and drove a few blocks away. I parked, shut the car off, and cried so hard that my stomach was sore the next day.

On the day of the audition, after a measly night of sleep, Ibo sat with me for over seven hours at the hotel where the audition was being held. I rehearsed my monologues and he acted as my hype man.

"Bro, that shit is so good, holy fuck!"

I needed the confidence because I was feeling the same nervousness I had felt at the New England football showcase. I felt everything was on the line, but there was peace that came with knowing that even if I wasn't accepted, I would still have a school I was enrolled in. My current school provided me with wonderful friends and a terrific education, even though something deep within told me I was not meant to be there long. I couldn't be certain of anything, and that in and of itself was nerve-wracking.

"You slept with my brother!"

"I trusted you!"

"How could you do this to me?"

"I'm sick! Can't you see that? You ignorant bastard!"

The screams of the other applicants' monologues pierced the barren silence of the waiting room where we sat waiting for our names to be called. Around the room, parents were sitting beside their kids, whispering words of affirmation and expressing their quiet notes of confidence in them.

A stockier middle-aged woman with short hair came out into the hallway, scarf high on her neck and wrapped below her defined chin. She reminded me of one of the friendlier librarians from my middle school, scanning the room briefly before she and I locked eyes. She smiled.

"Jet?"

I was up. I was ushered into the room and introduced to three other auditoners sitting at a table, just as it had been for my audition at Illinois, except this time the room was much smaller, and I had come prepared.

"Can I move this chair?" I asked.

"Sure. Whatever you need to do," the friendly librarian-type woman said with a therapeutic intonation.

I took a moment of stillness to myself before performing both monologues, one after the other, a few beats of silence in between to create separation.

When I was through, I smiled and thanked them for their time, walking out feeling fairly confident about what I had just done.

I returned to the waiting room and Ibo hadn't moved an inch but was watching as I approached with electric expectation and a juvenile eagerness in his eyes.

"Well? How'd it go, bro?"

"Honestly… I think pretty well."

He embraced me so hard it knocked both of us off balance, nearly sending us crashing into one of the parents waiting for their child.

CHAPTER 14

THIS HOME IS NO LONGER OURS

———

On my final day of freshman year, I decided to take one last walk around the campus and revel in all of its bustling green humidity before packing up my room.

My intuition told me I would not be back.

I was surprised by how moved I was from the thought of not returning. Taking a retrospective look at the year, like most others do when experiences come to an end, I was able to see just how important this year was for me. I could see this school, which I had once so stubbornly opposed and rebuked without warrant, had been an absolute privilege andundeniable blessing.

I packed my entire room into my car, said my farewells, and hit the highway heading toward a summer with no real agenda.

I did, however, know I would have to take care of some finalities for our home, which we had sold a month prior. I had not been back since the movers came to clear out the house, and it was my responsibility to make sure everything was looking up to snuff before the new owners moved in. I made sure the doors were locked, the lights were off, and that we hadn't accidentally left something behind in one of the covert spots where my mother liked to hide valuables. I would also need to clean the floors if, for some reason, they were dirty.

I also knew that Paris and I would have to begin checking off the list we had prayed would not need checking off—a list of our mother's instructions to be completed when her time was up, one that, despite our repudiation of it, she had thoroughly prepared us for.

It was a balmy afternoon in August, early evening creeping in over the rural naked highway my navigation system had selected to guide me home. Somewhere along this unbending route, I came to the decision that I would make the stop at my mother's house as soon as I arrived back into the north suburbs. Maybe I just wanted to get it over with, but I presume the truth was that deep down, even on a physiological level, I couldn't resist the impulse to stop "home" first.

I approached the front door of the house, but my nerves made it difficult to assert any kind of command over the door key; after a moment of honest effort, I found success and stepped in.

The house was startlingly warm, the kind of heavy insulated warmth that wood exudes, and the floors were spotless. The kitchen and living room were drenched in the light of the low sun seeping in through the windows. I'd never heard my feet traipse across the wood floor the way I did that afternoon; it was as though the house had stopped in time, holding its breath to listen as I explored the bare rooms. Each step echoed throughout this new, gaping vacancy our home had become. The house had been stripped and gutted, now an empty shell of a home pretending as though we had not, for years, offered it the sustenance of our lives.

I felt I was beginning to slowly drown in the silence of the house, or, at the very least, the floors had become quicksand and I was sinking into my own grief.

I eventually summoned the strength to walk up the stairs and into my mom's room, only to be brought to my knees. It was all gone—my mother and her room, the friends who came to the house on the weekends, and the home cooked meals. The life we all shared together was now, in a very authorized sense, finished.

Only the sun was there, reaching through her bedside window, to console me as I wept on the floor until I had not a tear left to give. I could not have anticipated the extent of pain this emptiness would bring, or the way it wrung my insides out like a wet towel.

In our yard, the grass bowed forward, swaying in the intermittent breeze as though in prayer. I closed my eyes for a moment and prayed I would open them to a full home again. I prayed everything that now seemed lost to my family would return to us. I prayed for healing, that the pain I felt would subside.

The tears I shed were left to soak into the wood of our floors, to be known and remembered by no one but me and this home. What seemed like an entire lifetime will go unknown to the very people who, in the upcoming weeks, will call this place home. The life my family and I shared there was packed up into boxes and stored, discarded, or sold.

I thought about how I would drive by the house slowly, somewhere down the road of time, glancing into the windows to see what it had become. A fleeting glimpse from the outside felt removed as I recalled even the most minor memories, like pulling up into the driveway and walking through the side door or taking my shoes off and placing them in a cubby. I had no choice but to capitulate to the reality of it all. This home was no longer ours.

Emotionally, I still carried around a heavy set of keys to the house, but soon I came to realize they seemed to only unlock the door to more sorrow.

From reading Eckhart Tolle, I knew what I had to do. I had to detach by relinquishing all sense of ownership and identification. I had to release my resistance to the direction in which I was now being guided toward. I needed to surrender to the present moment and all that came with it.[13] This would not be an easy task.

---

13   Tolle, Eckhart, *A New Earth: Awakening to Your Life's Purpose*, (New York: Penguin, 2016)..

In Eckhart Tolle's book *A New Earth*, he tells the story of two monks, Tanzan and Ekido, who were out for a walk. The anecdote—I will paraphrase—goes as follows:

It was morning. The streets were muddy and wet from the rain that came to town the night before. As the two monks walked toward their temple, they noticed a woman in a long, beautiful kimono. It was clear she needed to cross the street, but the mud was so deep she couldn't do so without getting her kimono filthy. Tanzan, wanting to help, walked over, lifted her up in his arms, and carried her across the street safely without muddying her garment. She thanked him and he then returned to Ekido's side; the two of them continued walking. Hours later, Ekido turned and said:

"Why would you do that? You picked that woman up even though you know that we, as monks, are not supposed to do things like that."

Tanzan replied calmly, "I put that woman down hours ago. Are you still carrying her?"[14]

For me, my home on Lorenzi Lane was the woman in a beautiful kimono; it was time to put her down and keep walking down the road.

After Paris and I finished up our move into my dad's house, I decided it would be best for me to get some kind of job. Ironically enough, I picked up a job as a delivery boy at the

---

14   Tolle, Eckhart, *A New Earth: Awakening to Your Life's Purpose*, (New York: Penguin, 2016)

same restaurant whose food we ate miserably the night after my mom passed away. I never liked their food, but the job was appealing because I had friends who were working there and because it was a mindless job that paid well and didn't require much effort. That was exactly what I felt I needed at the time.

I drove around in the summer heat with my shirt off and the windows down, going house to house—putting my shirt on once I stepped out of the car—delivering pizzas. It was perfect. I didn't mind that I sweat while wearing my uniform because the heat made me feel alive, as if I was doing honest, hard work.

For as long as I can remember, I've been infatuated with the idea of doing "honest work." A large part of me sought hard labor, where I would have to use my hands and build things and come home filthy from a day of the doing work everyone relies on, but most would never want to do themselves. This was the kind of work that felt good and pure—jobs that deserved a beer after long, arduous hours of work.

Instead, the most difficult task asked of me that summer was to load the pizzas into the pizza bag properly so they would not spill on the drive over to these houses that were always unreasonably difficult to find. These were houses that basic navigation systems couldn't detect. It seemed I was being sent to houses off of the grid, underground lairs, hideouts, and bomb shelters. Anyone living in places with fraudulent or nonexistent addresses needed pizza that summer. Come to think of it, maybe locating these caches was actually the hardest task required of me.

On this particular day, it was oppressively sultry. It was one of those days when the air conditioning and lighting units around the city were working at their maximum capacity, waning from the day's heat. I was inside the restaurant waiting for my next run when my boss grabbed me, pulled me aside, and told me solemnly to take off for the evening.

"Give your dad a call when you leave here."

I already knew, from the way he looked at me with commiserative eyes, what had happened.

In acting, we were taught to read subtext. To me, reading his was no challenge.

I walked out to my car and rang my dad up. With an unsteadiness in his voice, he confirmed my hunch that my grandma had passed way. I did not cry.

After hanging up, I sat there silently for a few minutes thinking about the life my grandma led, and the life she and I shared together. Somewhere at the front of my mind was also the piercing confusion at my lack of tears.

Maybe I felt relieved for my grandma because she would not have to live in the immobilizing pain she had been enduring for the handful of months prior. Maybe my new perspective on death had brought a sense of peace with it; sometime before this day, I had let go of the perception that death was the termination of all beings and began to acknowledge it as a graduation into the next life, a celebration of a life for what it is. I felt assured our loved ones do not just become lost or out of touch for the rest of our lives, but their life, rather, acts as a wave flowing back out to sea. The water does not die. Profoundly, it takes on a new form of being. It is eternally there.[15]

Maybe I found comfort in knowing my grandmother had been sleeping when she made her departure, leaving on the wings of a sweet dream. What I knew for certain was that I felt gladness in knowing she did not have to live anymore of her life stuck in a bed or through the dull blur of painkillers.

My grandma was, in a lot of ways, your stereotypical Jewish grandmother, although there is great discomfort that comes with using that word to describe her, because in more ways than not, she was anything but stereotypical.

She was a short, energetic women with blue-green eyes, strawberry blonde hair, and orange nails. I never saw her nails unpainted, and I never saw her nails be any other color than orange— it was her favorite color. She was an incredibly stylish woman who could always be seen in a pair of cool sneakers, clothes featuring cheetah print or some kind of luminous green design. She liked anything with bold colors, and she wore gold bracelets and gold rings—jewelry was central to her style. The bracelets jingled around her wrists and made it possible to hear her coming from far away.

From her clothes to her bright white teeth, my grandmother was a light beam of a woman.

---

15   Thich Nhat Hanh, *The Art of Living: Peace and Freedom in the Here and Now,* (New York: HarperCollins Publishers, 2017).

She seemed to get younger as the years went on, living as some kind of defiance to time, and her Jewishness was equally as unrelenting.

For those who do not know how a Jewish grandmother operates, you cannot fully understand them until you first understand their mission. Their mission is a direct result of the morals taught and ingrained in them from a young age. The traditional attributes of our grandmothers are as follows: selfless, fixative, affectionate, and, ultimately, a small but mighty heroic figure. They are the loving heart and soul of the family; they are comfort incarnate. And they never, I repeat *never*, let anyone else do the dishes in their own home.

With their mission comes the sense of obligation to make sure the family is overfed at all times and that there are leftovers—something to "nosh" on—in the fridge and pantry. It is rare for them to sit when meals are being served, and if they do, it is because they are begged by the rest of the family, finding satiation through watching others indulge in a meal they made. While everyone is eating, they are likely grabbing condiments or extra silverware, or prepping the dessert. They are also known to ask if anyone wants soup, or as my grandmother called it, "zoup," even if it's during the middle of summer. I would be willing to bet my entire life that at my grandma had noodle soup in her fridge at any given time.

Despite her resolute pleas for Paris and me to eat, we frequently had to politely, with love and persistence, decline. However, our resistance was only met with stronger persistence.

Her eventual capitulation was indicated by a sigh of disappointment and the offering of something else.

"What's wrong with you! You don't eat enough," she'd lament.

Let it be known that, to a Jewish grandmother, mine included, no one has ever really eaten enough. There were many times I was able to placate her, and in those instances, she was quick to offer validation.

When I fulfilled her expectations, she'd say, like a proud coach, "You did a good job, kid."

Needless to say, she took great pleasure in dropping off lunches for me during high school. She'd either pack an amalgamation of food from our local grocery store or get two sandwiches and a donut from my favorite local deli, leaving it with the security guards who manned the entrance office of our school. Without fail, the lunch would always have a note attached or written on the bag like a signed yearbook: "You better eat all of this. Have a great day! Love you! Grandma."

She would often bring food for the security guards as well to ensure they were properly fed. Every time I'd come in to grab my lunch, they would profess their love for her, and if a few weeks had gone by where she hadn't come to drop a lunch, they'd stop me as I walked into school with a comment like "Yo Jet! Where's grandma?" or "Is grandma coming by today?"

I appreciated how they said "grandma" and not "your grandma." I believe it illustrated the way our grandmothers seem to service the entire community and not just their own family. They treat all as their own. A grandmother often has many grandchildren over the course of her lifetime, not just those who share blood with her.

My grandma, very much like my father, did not complain. Her life was an unspoken dedication to selflessness, and I believe that because of this, she felt there was a deep and inherent wrongness to the idea of complaining. She believed complaining was an act of selfishness, therefore she refused to partake. She would not profess any sense of victimhood or declare herself more worthy of attention than someone else or express that, for one reason or another, she deserved better. Simply put, no matter how difficult it got, she did not subscribe to a life of caviling.

Even in her last few months, living in debilitating pain from the cervical cancer, she did not utter a grievance. She did, however, frequently apologize to me for having to drive her to the grocery store or for having to pick up food for her. The truth was that being able to reciprocate the love and unconditional generosity she had shown me my entire life was the greatest gift I could ask for—even though it was a gift that came with unfortunate consequences.

Eventually, she could no longer ride in the car with me, constrained to the living room couch that had become her new resting place because she no longer possessed the physical strength to get up the stairs to her room.

There is a poignancy that comes with having to watch someone who embodies qualities of great strength and vigor as they degenerate. It is kindred to the kind of torment found watching Superman being broken down by the power of kryptonite. The whole while you think, *No, this isn't right! Come on, get up! Get to your feet again!* It can be easy to forget even our superheroes share human qualities, that they too weaken under the pressure of forces bigger than themselves. Life, from time to time, reminds us of this—a painful yet divine reminder of the fragility of our being and of impermanence.

This kryptonite, the cancer, demonstrated its exertion on my grandmother in a way that seemed unusually abrupt to me.

Her last few weeks were enjoyed with milkshakes from her favorite local restaurant. She greatly appreciated their culinary touch of adding two small cookies on the straw. She felt this was a brilliant concept, and a style all restaurants should adhere to. These milkshakes were like prescription medicine for her—Oreo-flavored painkillers.

My grandmother spent many of her days "running around" as she called it. She ran errands, saw friends, and went for walks. She took care of whatever needed to be taken care of for the family—the more routine duties that amounted to a larger, greater function—working as the show runner behind the curtains. The benevolent matriarch who asked for nothing in return.

When I had seen her in the hospital, the day before I got the call of her passing, I noticed that for the first time, her nail polished was chipped.

CHAPTER 15

LET THERE BE REST

———

Sometimes, I imagine whatever may come after death as better than living here. I envision the complete and utter serenity and relief that must wash over our soul, freeing us from the weight of our pain and suffering, the lifting up and discarding of all anxieties and stress. An eternal state of equanimity.

Or, at the very least, maybe it would be better to live in another country. The quiet rolling greens of Tuscany or somewhere beside the serene whispers of the Mediterranean. Anywhere far from the violence and illness and anxiety endemic in our lives would be good—too much time spent here could drive the sensible into wild, dark places. I like to believe in the afterlife, after having been "good" here on earth, we are awarded with a life even fuller than the previous one, a life that knows no such thing as sickness or financial burdens or addiction or gloomy winters. In this life, people are not starving or living without a bed to sleep in, schools are not broken into by men with weapons, and people are not insulted for the color of their skin. There would be no such thing as loneliness or sorrow. There are certainly no divorces or funerals or riots. I believe you get the point. It is a life where people are loved and at ease.

I like to believe that this is how my family who has left this earth are already spending their afterlife.

There is so much to be dealt with during our lifetime. I'm aware of the ways suffering adds value to our lives—how it is one of our greatest teachers when it comes to the subjects of gratitude, perspective, and compassion—but there is certainly a threshold or chasm I slip into from time to time where we begin to only expect more suffering. We prepare ourselves for something even worse.

A "good day" transforms into its dark twin while on a phone call with my father as he expresses concerns about my brother. He tells me that he fears the idea, more than anything in life, that his four children will become three. He tells me he doesn't think he'd be able to survive that kind of pain. He covertly tells me he does not know how to cope with his lack of control over this particular situation.

A kid should listen to their father, he explains, as he has many times before, because the father brought that child into this world. Therefore, the child must afford their father the majority of jurisdiction when it comes to how they move forward in life—their decisions, romantic relationships, where they choose to live, admittance into a rehabilitation center.

I cannot blame my father for wanting to be the idealized version of the father he envisioned himself to be long before he had a diaper to change. I do not blame him for this, but the older I have gotten, the clearer it has become that there comes a time in a father's life, like there is for all of us, when he must surrender to the loss of control that takes place as his child grows up. My father has not quite made peace with this yet, instead resisting with a sizeable portion of his patriarchal might.

His fear begets my own. I begin to fear for myself and what my life would become if my dad were not around. How would I overcome that degree of pain, or warm myself to the frigid reality that I wouldn't have either parent to call or run home to?

I know plenty of people exist now as living answers to these questions, that people have lived through much worse and prospered—people who have found a source of God-like strength to tap into profound resilience and perseverance.

When my mind wanders to these darker places, I remind myself that these thoughts are rooted in the ego. The ego tells me to choose to live in fear, while my true consciousness tells me to choose to live out of love. I notice when I choose love, I am brought back to my trust in life, and I can again sense within me the basic goodness we are all born with. When we choose to live out of love, we do not attach ourselves to persistent anxiety or daily stress and instead meet them with acceptance and let them pass along without having to make them ours. When we choose love, we let life guide the way gracefully, free from our egoic tendency to resist the purity and perfection of the Now.

When I choose love, I am overcome by a sense of faith that my brother will find clarity and not look back. I regain trust that my father will be well.

I ask The Universe for a hand, but I know It has already made a plan for all of this. I trust It, but I also understand that my trust will not necessarily yield a desirable outcome. I have seen how The Universe works and taken note over the years; It will act how It must, making sense of it all later on. The Universe will ensure that the puzzle pieces of life fall together, sometimes creating a rather tragic picture, other times composing something more beautiful than anticipated.

Either way, it is on us to make peace with the reality that we are not the ones doing the piecing together. It is our responsibility to not judge these pieces as they fall before us but to be aware of their impermanence and accept with joy and composure whatever the outcome may be.

Such is the challenge of life. Moment after moment we watch the pieces as they present themselves, observing with fascination or excitement or concern or delight the way they are moved to fit into the perfectly crafted story of our lives. It is both a process and a journey.

Those who resist this process, as I have, often kick and scream and throw tantrums, and behind tears they give fractured speeches about unfairness. They cling to the past, as I have, carrying the weight of the past down the capricious road of life, and wear themselves down without even realizing it.

Everyone's reaction to the present moment, or the "is-ness" of life, is unique, but if we look closely, we see clearly those who resist are met with a greater force of resistance and those who succumb amicably to the Now are met with greater strength and mindfulness. Those who make peace with the present are treated as a dear friend, but those who choose not to foster such a relationship become adversarial. The beauty is we always have a choice in this matter.

After I hung up the phone with my father, I thought of calling my brother but didn't. I sat there, eyes closed, envisioning myself breathing in his suffering and breathing out my love for him. I prayed that he would feel it.

CHAPTER 16

CELL SERVICE

It was a beautiful Friday in Los Angeles. The February sun, as if renewed by the new year, was unusually warm in the cloudless sky.

I was hanging around my apartment, the sunlight reaching through our sliding door and painting swaying shadows on the floor of the palm trees that surround our patio.

I had just finished meditating, as I sometimes like to do, on the living room couch—seated on a pillow, legs crossed, hands out and open, eyes closed.

As soon as I close my eyes to begin meditation, there are typically throngs of thoughts that spring into mind as though they had been lying in wait. These thoughts arrive like paparazzi, ruthless and pervading the inner calm of my consciousness with their boisterous buzz. I feel that it's rather easy to buckle under the pressure of the discomfort they bring.

I often recall a commercial I once saw that almost perfectly exemplifies this experience.

The commercial I'm referring to happens to be an advertisement for Beats by Dre headphones showing Colin Kaepernick, renowned former quarterback for the San Francisco 49ers, pulling up to a rivaling team's stadium on the day of the game.[16]

As the 49ers' team bus enters the lot, there are seemingly thousands of rivaling fans standing out in the pouring rain shouting insults at him over the security fences which, judging by the fans' blazing vehemence, seem to be the only thing restraining them from actually leaping at the bus in effort to assault him.

The bus comes to a halt, the fans still screaming and throwing all kinds of objects at his window, aggressions now louder than before. Yet Colin's disposition is as calm as ever. Before he gets up from his seat, he places his headphones over his ears and the world falls completely silent. He selects a song from his phone—"I'm The Man" by Aloe Blacc is now the only thing he can hear—and steps off the bus, making his way through the crowd who taunts him like insolent children do to zoo animals. Carrying himself with unwavering composure, he is unfazed by the clamor or the rain pouring down on him.

Soon Colin is in the players tunnel, which leads to the team locker room, and is removed from the chaos. A serene smile

---

16   Beats by Dre, "Hear What You Want," (YouTube, 2014).

finds his face; the camera cuts to him completely alone in a training room where he's stretching, preparing for the game ahead. The commercial concludes a few moments after the slogan is seen superseded on the screen: "Hear What You Want."

I do my best to channel this energy, envisioning Kaepernick as my poised consciousness and the feral fans as all other thoughts, distractions, and egoic demands. I remind myself the fans are not an extension of myself, the noise and presence of the crowd is impermanent and fleeting, so there is no reason to expend energy on reacting to them. Remaining present, concentrating on the equanimity of the Now, all distractions begin to strip away and I am left alone in the beautiful company of my own breath and beating heart. At this moment, I find profound joy, and like Kaepernick, I can't help but smile.

During my meditation that day, I was gifted with the pleasant thought that my mom was just in the other room. This was the first time after she had passed away that I actually felt her presence. It wasn't the feeling that she was holding my hand, hugging me, or anything overwhelmingly physical, but it was the sense that she was doing work on her desktop in the other room as she often did at home. I felt for the first time that she was home with me, so much so I could recall her smell—the floral undertones and the ocean-like salinity of her essential oils—so vividly it became real. I began to tear up during meditation because of how incredible and soothing this felt.

After two years, I felt I was back with my mother again.

I thought it would only be appropriate I receive this sense of her presence as a partial sign to clean my apartment, knowing she always liked the house spotless and I did not want her to see my place in its current slovenly condition. So, I began to sweep, as she had taught me to, and wipe down the counters with a wet and soapy cloth, as she had taught me to, and make my bed and fold my clothes, as she taught me to. I cleaned my apartment and felt her hands and spirit work through mine. It was as though we were cleaning together, or maybe she was cleaning through me—which, knowing her, would make more sense.

While folding my clothes, my phone began to ring from where it was charging in the kitchen. I walked over to see my mom was calling me.

Immediately, my entire body was awash with chills. Seeing my phone say "Mom" as it rang gave my soul enough nourishment to survive peacefully for a lifetime. I took this moment as a powerful sign, enjoying the experience of my phone's buzzing more than I ever had.

I let the phone ring for a bit longer before deciding to quench the anticipation that there would be an automated voice on the other end saying something I already knew, like the number had already been disconnected.

I slid to answer, put the phone to my ear, and listened a moment. Silence.

"Hello?" I asked instinctively.

Silence.

"Ma, is this you calling me?" I said with a smile, now joking around like I had caught on to a friend prank calling me, but I could also feel the chills begin to run through me once again.

On the other end, a gentle static flared that after a moment was pierced by a soft female voice:

"Hello?" I could just barely hear her on the other end.

"Hello? Mom?" I said desperately, like Winona Rider in *Stranger Things* when she's trying to contact her missing son.[17]

I felt like I could reach my arm out and pull my mother back down to earth; I felt that I was close to something tangible and in the presence of a force much bigger than myself.

The voice on the other end offered one more tender "hello" before it was drowned out by static; the call was disconnected.

I tried to call back several times, but it wouldn't even ring.

Obviously, I tried to make sense of this experience.

I could clearly remember a conversation I had with my mother's dear friend and spiritual guide, Mariana, the week before.

---

17   Matt Duffer and Ross Duffer, *Stranger Things: Chapter 1: The Vanishing of Will Byers,* (Albuquerque, NM: Netflix, 2016. TV).

She had told me not to be afraid to ask my mom for a sign but mentioned that if I was going to ask, then I must be willing and ready to receive it. She told me to be patient and not turn a blind eye on The Universe or grow disheartened if a sign doesn't come immediately. When we bow our heads in dismay, we miss the beauty of what is right before us.

Inspired by this conversation, I had decided to write my mom a letter the day after Mariana and I spoke and asked my mother for a sign she was still with me.

I hadn't included a postal address, but the letter seemed to have found her just fine. I like to believe that when it did, she reached for the phone.

CHAPTER 17

WITH MY FEET, YOU MAY WALK

———

I came home somewhere in the middle of March for spring break. It had been a cold and gray week back home for the most part, but the weekend was predicted to bring nicer weather.

Just having finished up a workout, I ran into my mom's ex-boyfriend Tim in the gym locker room. He had put on a significant amount of weight, his pallor face now supporting dark bags around his eyes like he hadn't slept in weeks.

This was the first time I felt real empathy for him. My heart understood his pain. We exchanged a greeting, but he barely registered my presence. I asked him how things were. He did his best to sell me the "things are fine" charade, but it was obvious that he was anything but fine.

The conversation had ended only moments after it began, but I gave him a brief and awkward embrace before I left because

I felt this was an opportunity for reconciliation, and because by now I knew that the power of forgiveness would overcome all else. He offered a weak, sedated smile in return, and we parted ways.

Later that week, when we finally saw some warmth and sunshine, I felt the impulse to revisit Lorenzi Lane. Soon, I found myself wandering the perimeters of the house after learning the people who lived there now were away on vacation.

Looking at the house now, it was as though it was entirely different—as though this were only a replica of the one I knew. I felt the dualism of nostalgia, which purports ideas like, *"It's as if this all happened a lifetime ago,"* and the contrary, *"It's as if this only happened yesterday."* I didn't know which side to agree with, so I stood in the middle of them both.

In the backyard, the lawn chairs stared at one another blankly and the tiles on the patio lay face up soaking in the sun that laid across their chests. The tiles prayed for warmer days so they could feel the smooth tiptoeing of bare feet once more. The grass prayed for a summer breeze so it could sway like a soulful chorus group, the way it's known to do this time of year. The trees surrounding the yard, their branches reaching out in a familial manner, confessed that they were sure they'd never see me again. The sliding door said nothing.

I took a few more moments to stand there listening and breathing before I departed with a smile, filled to the brim with gratitude for the years I shared there and for the life before me now. I made my way to the same path my mother and I used to walk together.

As soon as I passed the gate that signifies the start of the path, I noticed that my pace was a little too fast. I slowed down because I didn't want to miss anything. The air was delicate and smelled of the transition between winter and spring; this smell brings immense hope and reward with it.

It whispers affirmations with great enthusiasm: "*Yes, you've made it through another winter. Your prize will be here shortly.*"

I love the perennial promises this time of year makes, and the way all life becomes revitalized. The last remnants of snow cling to dead leaves, the trees stand around patiently for their summer coats, the scent of wet soil on hills swear to you that their brown flesh will soon turn green, the nude pavement lays bare, and the shadows of tree branches endeavor to grab one another from across the way.

I stopped in my place and turned around to face the sun. I let out a deep exhale, "Ahhhhhh," and the wind blew its chilly breath back at me. The birds sung, encouraging the sun to keep holding me and to warm the roots once again. I held my stare and I was flooded with a sense of remarkable strength as my feet began to feel as though someone was planting them deep into the ground.

After a minute or so, I turned back around and continued toward the water. The man and his beagle were not there that day. I only saw one person on my way down to where the frigid sand awaited, but he was walking the opposite way. He was much older and had been dressed warmer than I was. He walked slowly with his hands held behind his back, and as we crossed each other, he looked up, both of us exchanging amiable smiles.

"How are ya?" I asked almost exactly at the same time that he had said, "Hi there."

I thought for a bit about whether or not he typically walked this path alone, or if he also had a friend or wife or grand-child who walked beside him, and, if so, where they were that day.

My nose had become runny by the time I got down to the water where the wind was significantly stronger. Now the waves did not kiss the rocks, but rather hurled themselves forward with innocent aggression. Water flung and spit into anything it could find, and I sat on a large rock that over-looked all of it and just watched. The first half of the water was incredibly light blue. I wasn't sure how, thinking maybe it was the sun's doing, the darkness of the back portion of the lake interrupted the lighter shade of the water at a single, definitive point without the hues blending.

The limitlessness of the water and the way it met the sky at the very back of the lake's throat was forever the same. I closed my eyes to the sounds of the water screaming with excitement and gave my thoughts over to The Universe for a moment. I expressed my gratitude for the day before me and the sun above, for the love of my family and friends, for our health, for nineteen full years shared with my mother, and for the knowledge that she would forever be with me. I gave thanks for the unadulterated guidance and support, and for putting me where I was supposed to be in this world.

I opened my eyes and watched the water until I saw a plane fly over thousands of feet above, creating a trail of white streaks in the sky. I wondered if the pilot was able to see me from up there, if maybe he was able to intercept my prayers and fly them directly up somewhere higher and let them go for all to hear.

Soon, I stopped wondering and made my start back to where I'd come from. I felt much warmer now, my legs still fresh, walking face to face with the sun. I felt as though the height of my shoulders aligned with the tops of the trees. I smiled because all of this was familiar and beautiful. I could picture my mom asking me about my plans for the summer and saying she would love to see me start auditioning for commercials or enroll in a stand-up comedy class, but only as long as I worked plenty of jokes about her into my set.

I could picture her walking beside me in a pair of bright yoga pants with her arms pumping and doing those short, snare-drum-like exhales she liked to let out with each swing of her arm, only this time I wouldn't tease her for it. Eventually, she would put her arm through mine and lean her head on my shoulder as we walked, not because she was tired or needed assistance, but because she loved being able to hold her tall baby boy.

I passed many people on my way back, and some stared at me with faint commiseration and smiles that said, "*What are you doing walking alone?*"

I smiled back, assuring them that I wasn't.

CHAPTER 18

LET'S START WITH THE LIVING ROOM

———

Each time I returned from school, I was reminded of all the complications that interfered with my idea of home. What I knew to be home no longer seemed to exist. Like hermit crabs searching for a new shell, Paris and I did our best to adjust somewhere new while our sense of home experienced a rather significant metamorphosis.

This new shell became our father's house, or as I like to call it "Studio 55": a small, two-story house my father covered every inch of with artwork and his own notes for desirable renovation on the walls, typically in sharpie. There are also magazine pages, printed pictures, and color strips tacked onto the walls to give himself more concrete conceptual ideas for the house. In the kitchen hangs a vision board with more pictures and notes tacked onto things. This is a household, as you can now imagine, where things aree tacked to other things to hang for years on end.

The kitchen, like most things in the house, isn't entirely comprehensive—or maybe the word I'm looking for is "traditional"—but I attribute this to my father not being accustomed to having to do anything domestic for himself; he never had to actually decorate a home, cook, clean, grocery shop, or do his own laundry because there was a team of people, including my mother, who did it for him. There were people hired to take care of such things.

However, he was now learning to do the things my mother had taught Paris and I to do years ago. He's still in the early phases of his education in domestic work, but he's a quick learner. Granted, there's still a sofa, chair, and a rug in the back of the kitchen, small tables placed throughout the house like some kind of obstacle course, and many things leaning against the walls. This is one of his favorite strategies—if something is too big for a tac, it gets leaned against the wall. Nevertheless, he is learning enthusiastically.

On the other hand, my mother kept our home spotless. You couldn't leave a cup on the counter without it being removed and washed minutes later, followed by a wipe down of the entire counter. In my mother's home, I was admonished for touching the doors or walls with dirty hands, or for leaving my shoes on the wrong mat. Her home was manicured, perfectly organized, and almost always gleaming with cleanliness.

Disparities like this made the transition into my father's house rather unsettling. There were times when I did not feel comfortable returning home during our academic breaks, but December brought the holidays and my father's birthday, and it wouldn't be right to let him celebrate without me there.

"Well, dad, what do you wanna do for your big day?"

It was his birthday and he and I were the only one's home. Paris no longer had winter break because she had begun a career in Vermont.

"Uhhh.. I don't know, J.E.T. Let's do some brainstorming!"

We threw some ideas around, limited by circumstances like the fact that it was a Sunday in the middle of December in Chicago. We eventually landed on the idea to test drive one of the Ferrari's at the dealership a few towns over. Secretly, I liked the idea because I was still attached to the fantasy of getting our old life back, including the valuables we owned.

If you've seen Spielberg's *Catch Me If You Can* starring young Leo DiCaprio as Frank Abagnale Jr., then you're familiar with how Frank Jr. seeks to reclaim the life he felt was taken from him and his family. His mother and father divorced after his dad, once an esteemed man of the New Rochelle Rotary Club and a local shop owner, was targeted by the IRS and forced to give up their family's affluent lifestyle.

Frank Abagnale Jr. persistently reassures his father, who is played brilliantly by Christopher Walken, he's going to "get it all back," including reparations to his father and mother's marriage. In the end, he cannot. Frank Jr. has run from the police, lied, and stolen in nearly every state in America in an effort to escape the reality of his new life, unwilling to let go of the way things were.

After all his running and hiding, he is exhausted and afraid, wanting the chase to be over with. His stamina is at its wits end, but he does not have a choice. He can't call it quits because there's an entire FBI unit after him.

This is how pain and suffering catch up to us when we do not address it. All of us can only run and hide for so long before we find ourselves caught.

I wanted to see my dad get the nice cars and the nice house and the vacations and the beautiful wife back. In unspoken longing, I wanted these things more than I'd like to admit to myself. Many times, I thought of becoming wealthy and buying it all back for us. From time to time, I imagined how that could become a great source of healing for us.

In keeping with the reference, I liken this vision of mine to the scene when Frank Jr., months after being on the run and millions of stolen dollars later, takes his father to an upscale restaurant for lunch. The two of them sit there across from one another, Frank Jr. in his faux pilot's uniform and Frank Sr. in one of his old, expensive suits—an emblem I believe was utilized to spotlight the difference between the life Frank Sr. once led and the life he led now.

While the appearance of the suit and the man who wears it may remain unchanged, the man is not.

In the scene, Frank Jr. slides his father a small box with a ribbon on it across the table.

"You know what those are right? Those are the keys to a 1965 Cadillac DeVille convertible. Brand-new, Dad. Red with white interior split seats, air conditioning, the works."

"Are you giving me a Cadillac?"

"Yeah. I'm giving you a Cadillac. Dad, she's parked downstairs. When we're done eating lunch why don't you, you know, drive on over to mom's house, pick her up, take a little joy ride?"

"Do you know what would happen if the IRS found out I was driving around in a new coupe? I took the train here, Frank. I'm taking the train home."

"Alright. I have plenty of money. You know, if you ever need anything…"

"You worried? About me?"

"No, I'm not… I'm not worried."

"You think I can't buy my own car? Two mice fell into a bucket of cream, Frank. Which one am I?"

"You're that second mouse," referring to the speech his father gave upon being honored as a lifetime member at the New Rochelle Rotary Club.[18]

"Two little mice fell in a bucket of cream. The first mouse quickly gave up and drowned. The second mouse wouldn't quit. He struggled so hard that eventually he churned that cream into butter and crawled out. Gentleman, as of this moment, I am that second mouse."[19]

My father, like Frank Sr., is that second mouse.

He and I pulled up to the dealership, but the building lights were off. Soon, we discovered the doors were also locked. The dealership was closed—neither of us had thought to call in beforehand. We looked in through the windows, hands over our foreheads, and pressed against the glass gently to block out the glare of daylight, surveying the collection of idle, tantalizing cars.

"Is there another dealership around here?" I asked.

"No, but that's alright. C'mon, let's go grab a bite and go home. I got the perfect movie for us."

I took a deep breath and acquiesced, disheartened that the plan had fallen through. Back at home, he and I hopped on

---

18   Steven Spielberg, *Catch Me If You Can,* (Glendale, CA: DreamWorks Pictures, 2002. DVD).

19   Ibid.

the couch and threw some blankets on to fight the chill of our living room.

We turned on a French film with a title I can't remember, and a few minutes into the movie he held my hand in his—even though Paris and I were older now, he still liked to hold our hands. Neither of us mind it.

"Thank you," he said through a deep exhale of sincerity.

"Sure, dad. I'm sorry we couldn't do something more fun, but tomorrow we will."

"Are you kidding? I'm here watching a movie with my son. I couldn't ask for more. You know, going over there today made me realize I really don't need any of that. I wanted to take one of those cars out because I thought it would make me feel good, you know? But I don't need it. This is what I needed."

In that moment, I could feel a part of the me who wanted it all back—the part that felt lust for the cars we had just seen—dissolve.

There, on the couch with my father, I remember being overcome by the realization that what was once referred to as dad's house had now become home.

This home, with encouragement from Paris and I, had been put up for sale. My father, for a while, hadn't been able to find a job that suited him around the area, so we began discussing the idea of him moving elsewhere. For a while, my father met our furtherance on this matter with unwavering protest. It became clear and entirely understandable that he was deeply uncomfortable with moving away from the place in which he had created a life and family for himself. To leave the state of Illinois would be, to a large extent, a departure from who he is now, and certainly a departure from who he was. He would not be able to take the baggage from all of his previous years with him to somewhere new. It would be impossible to carry.

Eventually, my father's stubbornness abated, and he agreed to listing the house for sale.

One often does not realize the extent of what they have accumulated from over the years until it is time to pack and clean up.

"Jet, I'm gonna need your help tidying up the house today before the realtor gets here."

As he and I began tidying, it became unsettlingly obvious just how much, for lack of a better term, garbage was around the house—pages from magazines, old letters that had never even been opened, pictures of people we didn't even know, dog leashes, Christmas cards, old clothes, shopping bags that once carried those clothes, unidentified wires for unidentified electronics, and all other imaginable and totally unnecessary items. Some things were dusty or broken or hanging on by a thread. I could sense my dad becoming gradually more overwhelmed as we worked through the house.

When the realtor finally came, after touring the house for about an hour, she began to note everything that needed reparations. The knobs needed fixing, the walls needed painting, the floors needed a cleaning, and the many things needed removal. All the while, my father would match her notes with justifications of his own vision for the house.

My father, tirelessly, seems to have visions. Everywhere he goes, he's taking pictures of buildings or houses for sale or artwork or antique chairs, pulling pages out from magazines and books and birthday cards. He finds inspiration in things most people don't even bother to look at.

This realtor did not, however, share these visions with him. What she shared with him was the reality of what she had just seen, and the pragmatic requisites for restoration.

My dad took a long, deep breath, smiled and thanked her sincerely for taking the time to come by.

After she had left, my dad sat down on the couch, letting out an exhalation of exhaustion.

"Jesus, Jet. How did I let this happen?"

"What?"

"I have all this shit around the house that's just been piling up and I've been living with it like this. I'm sickened by myself."

I looked at him, sitting back on the couch, with his glasses in one hand and his face held in his other. He only does this expression when he's truly exhausted.

If it were a game of poker, this would be his tell: he takes his glasses off and rubs his eyes and face with both hands before holding his head for a few moments.

When he takes his glasses off, I can see his eyes in a way I seldom get to see. I can see what he's seen and the way these experiences have created a tenebrous weight underneath his eyes. I'm always taken back by this, sometimes having forgotten just how much this man, my father, has been through—how much he has carried throughout his lifetime for himself and his family, and how many hours he's spent awake doing just that. I can see in his eyes the many nights he couldn't sleep and the countless days he's spent summoning the strength to keep his legs and heart moving forward the way he does.

I knew in a few more moments, if I didn't say something to him while he's sitting there on the couch, he'll fall asleep.

"Dad."

"Yeah," he said as though he were not falling asleep.

"Let's start with the living room."

He opened his eyes, sat up, put his glasses back on, and took a deep breath.

"Okay. Let's do it, kid."

CHAPTER 19

CAP AND GOWN

———

I'm mere weeks away from my college graduation, a day spoken about with thick, anticipative tones of finality—not too dissimilar, as I see it, from the way people speak of death.

At this time, it is much more frequent that my ego arises, demanding I concern myself with both the past and the future. It makes assertions about different linear paths to follow and whispers fearful thoughts about having to leave school, friends, and this current version of myself. Ultimately, my ego wants to strip me from the Now and bare-knuckle brawl with the reality of what is.

I remind myself of the profound words written by Eckhart Tolle:

"The decision to make the present moment into your friend is the end of the ego."[20]

---

20 Eckhart Tolle, *A New Earth: Awakening to Your Life's Purpose*, (London: Penguin, 2016).

I can feel when the relationship between myself and the Now becomes dysfunctional. I have noticed how conflict arises from judging, resisting, or attaching to life.

I remind myself time and time again to sit with whatever arises with acceptance and impartial observance until it passes.

I remind myself that I cannot force an agenda on life, and that there is no value in blurring the Now with distractions from my past or visions of the future.

I remind myself there is inherent beauty in uncertainty, and that it often becomes a window for divine opportunities.

I remind myself operating from a place of fear is intrinsically egoic, whereas choosing to operate from a place of love, as we all know how to do, reveals our truest self.

I remind myself to thank each moment and to search for appreciation even in the most painful or seemingly mundane of times, opening my heart so that I may receive with gratitude the gifts of life, especially those gifts that I too often take for granted, such as my ability to walk to school.

Last semester, I was practicing a walking meditation while on my way back from class, a practice I had heard Thich Nhaht Hanh speak about. The practice is very simple: it asks that you slow down your walking to a pace that you can match each inhale and exhale with a step forward. On each inhale you think or say to yourself "I have arrived," and on the exhale you think or say "I am home."[21] By tuning into the sound and rhythm of our breathing, rooting each foot deeper into earth, we are brought back to a stunning clarity of consciousness.

After a few minutes of practicing this meditation, I found myself so overtaken by gratitude that tears of joy began running down my face. I felt deeply that, after being away for what felt like an eternity, I was home again.

I later read an article written by Thich Nhat Hanh on the practice, wanting to know more about why I was able to feel this way. I found exactly what I had been looking for. In the article he wrote:

"We may have run all our life, but now we don't have to run anymore. This is the time to stop running. To be grounded in the earth is to feel its solidity with each step and know that we are right where we are supposed to be...Breathe, take a mindful step, and arrive. We are already at home."[22]

While this was a lesson for me about cherishing even the moments I often considered inconsequential, it was also a realization that it's very possible, and within our nature, to find a profound sense of home in the Now, even while I was thousands of miles away from my family.

21 Thich Nhat Hanh, *The Art of Living: Peace and Freedom in the Here and Now,* (New York: HarperCollins Publishers, 2017).

22 Thich Nhat Hanh, "Thich Nhat Hanh on Walking Meditation," (Lion's Roar, May 31, 2019).

As my sense of home grew deeper and more expansive, so did my appreciation for my home in Chicago. I soon found the apprehension I once felt about returning home to Studio 55 had been assuaged and transmuted into enthusiasm and joy rather than discomfort.

Now, at home stretched out above the couch in the living room, is a work of art that my mother gifted my father as an anniversary present many years ago. The work is a collection of letters, crafted from faux red roses, that reads, "Life Goes On."

The sunlight comes through the low windows of the living room, reflecting off of the pavement outside and illuminating the red of the flowers in a way that seems to bring them to life, permeating our home with their radiance.

I'm fond of this piece because it serves as a stunning reminder: however each moment presents itself when it arrives at our door—whether our ego deems it to be good, bad, ugly, painful, gorgeous, or cathartic—and whatever it is we are destined to endure and celebrate, each one of these moments are only temporary.

We must understand and trust that the moment has come for a specific and inherently perfect reason, that we thank it for coming all this way to visit and we must—without having judged, reacted harshly, or identified with whatever the moment may or may not have brought with it—carry onward freely, bettered by it.

Let us commit to moving along on our journey one step at a time, each step more courageous than the last. Let us put our faith and love into life, unconcerned with our destination.

CHAPTER 20

LOOK CLOSELY, WE'LL BE ALRIGHT

———

When the house my family shared was no longer ours, I, like the rest of my family, could not fathom the direction in which life would move us.

There was simply no way to know, just as I have not the slightest idea as to where the photograph that hung in our old living room wound up, or where it will wind up in the years to come.

For as long as we lived in that house, I did not understand my father's affection for it.

Recently, however, I asked him what it was about the photo that appealed to him.

He pulled his phone out and Googled a picture of it, zooming in with his fingers to enlarge its details.

"Here. Look right there," he told me, pointing to a small area of the photo.

After a few moments of looking, he followed up, "Do you see it?"

In the background of the photo, somewhere in the shallow region of the ocean, there was what looked to be some kind of outlet that had been painted over.

It wasn't an outlet. My father explained that—as can be seen more clearly when in front of the actual, physical work—the small rectangular rise in the water fractures the verisimilitude of the photo and is where the woman's safety cable is hooked into.

He explained that, if you look closely enough, you can see a wall cable attached to the back of her jeans, creating the appearance that she is being fiercely pulled at by the storm.

"I loved that," my father said.

"At first you're uneasy looking at the photo. You fear for the family. But after a few moments of really looking, you realize that it's only a set. This whole scene has been designed and staged to perfection by something bigger than these people. Realizing this, there comes a wonderful sense of assurance that this family is, and will be, just fine."

ACKNOWLEDGMENTS

I'd like to acknowledge those who have given this book, and the stories within it, the legs to run:

The Fishbein Family, The Maggos Family, The Fleisher Family, The Singer Family, Caroline Nutt & The Nutt Family, The Robbins Family, The Schneider Family, The Lepp Family, The D'Alba Family, The Volpentesta Family, The Bardi Family, The Green Family, Suzi Escobar-Kenyon, Estelle Walgreen, Ibrahim Sare, Ricky Leme, Carlos Benitez, Dylan Gold, Ron Suber, Mariana Krstevski, Nate Guadagni, Brad Gerber, Eric Koester, Jordan Waterwash, and Ryan Porter.

I'd also like to gratefully acknowledge:

Jack Appelbaum, Noah Jacobs, Mars Zeng, Mitchell Lee, Hwoo Lee, Patrick O'Reilly, Antonio Mauri, Mara Lorin, Alex Nordstrom, Nate Aframian, Ben Refoua, Clare Chandler, Marjorie Williams, Cory Bennett, Tony Barrios, Dom Haubner, Ford Johnstone, Jake Durburg, Jake Cirame, The Coughlin Family, Taylor Kuchman, Kelly Burson, Leah Chung, Ryan Rogers, Ryan Goldsher, Eitan Senerman, Chris

Boyd, Diego Riley, Jed Rutstein, Corey Goldglit, Michael Prostran, Camille Henderson, Melissa Merritt, The Tornes Family, Tommy Chandler, Spencer Dowell, Jonathon Levin, Kevin Wu, David 'Bernie' Bernstein, Chase Nathan, Josh Silverstein, Brian Zhuang, Nick Shanks, Patrick Kawakami, Jordan Rao, Alain Carles, Adam Sraberg, UIUC Pike, Aly Olvera, Amber Orradre, Sean McGroarty, Ryan Porter, and Anthony Thomas.

Lastly, I'd like to acknowledge a few sources of inspiration:

Dave Eggers, Eckhart Tolle, Pema Chödrön, Thich Nhat Hanh, James Baldwin, Julie Price, Judi Elman, and Aubrey 'Drake' Graham.

APPENDIX

———

AUTHOR'S NOTE:

Tolle, Eckhart. *A New Earth: Awakening to Your Life's Purpose.*
New York: Penguin, 2016.

CH. 1:

Nicosia, Nic. *"Near Modern Disaster #8."* MutualArt (1984): *https://
www.mutualart.com/Artwork/Near-Modern-Disaster---8/
E4D17B2C508F333E*

CH. 6:

Chodron, Pema. *Welcoming the Unwelcome: Wholehearted Living
in a Brokenhearted World.* Boulder: Shambhala, 2019.

Tolle, Eckhart. *A New Earth: Awakening to Your Life's Purpose.*
New York: Penguin, 2016.

CH. 7:

McKay, Adam, dir. *Anchorman: The Legend of Ron Burgundy.*
Glendale, CA: DreamWorks Pictures, 2004. DVD.

CH. 8:

Patrick Shanley, John. *Prodigal Son.* New York: Theatre Communications Group, 2016.

Weir, Peter, dir. *Dead Poets Society.* Burbank, CA: Touchstone Pictures, 1989. DVD.

CH. 9:

Chödrön, Pema. *"Tonglen: Bad In, Good Out."* Lion's Roar (December 6, 2019): *https://www.lionsroar.com/tonglen-bad-in-good-out-september-2010/*

Drake, Vocalist, *"Practice,"* by Drake. Track #17 on *Take Care*: Young Money & Cash Money Records, 2011.

Nolan, Christopher, dir. *Interstellar.* Los Angeles, CA: Paramount Pictures, 2014, DVD.

CH. 14:

Nhat Hanh, Thich. *The Art of Living: Peace and Freedom in The Here and Now.*

New York: HarperCollins Publishers, 2017.

Tolle, Eckhart. *A New Earth: Awakening to Your Life's Purpose.* New York: Penguin, 2016.

CH. 16:

Beats by Dre. *"Hear What You Want."* YouTube, 2:47 (January 13, 2014): *https://www.youtube.com/watch?v=2-j4n-sna6Y*

Duffer, Matt and Ross Duffer, dir. *Stranger Things: Chapter 1: The Vanishing of Will Byers.* Albuquerque, NM: Netflix, 2016. TV.

CH. 18:

Spielberg, Steven, dir. *Catch Me If You Can.* Glendale, CA: Dream-Works Pictures, 2002. DVD.

CH. 19:

Nhat Hanh, Thich. "*Thich Nhat Hanh on Walking Meditation.*" Lion's Roar (May 31, 2019): *https://www.lionsroar.com/how-to-meditate-thich-nhat-hanh-on-walking-meditation/*

Nhat Hanh, Thich. *The Art of Living: Peace and Freedom in The Here and Now.* New York: HarperCollins Publishers, 2017.

Tolle, Eckhart. *A New Earth: Awakening to Your Life's Purpose.* New York: Penguin, 2016.

Made in the USA
Coppell, TX
21 August 2020

33928292R00128